ASK ME OUT

Series Editor: Rony Robinson

Hodder & Stoughton
LONDON SYDNEY AUCKLAND TORONTO

Acknowledgements

The Publishers would like to thank the following for permission to reproduce material in this volume:

The Independent for the review of *Love and Truffles* from the Independent; The Scotsman for the review of *Love and Truffles* from The Scotsman, September 1988; Time Out Ltd for the review of *Love and Truffles* from Time Out, 6th April 1989; What's On in London for the review of *Love is a Sweet Thing* from What's On and Where To Go in London, 6th April 1989.

Every effort has been made to trace and acknowledge ownership of copyright. The Publishers will be glad to make suitable arrangements with any copyright holders whom it has not been possible to contact.

British Library Cataloguing in Publication Data
Ask me out. – (Upstage series)
I. Robinson, Rony II. Series
822

ISBN 0-340-50856-6

First published 1991

Typeset by Litho Link Limited, Leighton, Welshpool, Powys, Wales.
Printed in Great Britain for Hodder and Stoughton Educational, a division of Hodder and Stoughton Ltd, Mill Road, Dunton Green, Sevenoaks, Kent by Clays Ltd, St Ives PLC

Contents

LOVE AND TRUFFLES *Mike Harris*		1
TRAPPIN'	*Frances McNeil*	43
DON'T CRY BABY	*Katie Campbell*	89
Activities		134

Scene One

Cue factory whistle, MABEL *and* CAROL *clock in.* HARRY *watches, fingering watch.*

CAROL *(Punching card.)* Mornin', Mabel.

MABEL *(Punching card.)* What's good about it? Turn that bleedin' thing off, will you?! *(Factory whistle ends abruptly.)* Stinkin' head.

HARRY C'mon girls; Bloody hell!

MABEL Ten seconds to lift off Harry. *(Taking up position on line next to Carol.)* An' who the hell are you callin' a girl, anyhow? Old enough to be your mistress. What d'you reckon, Carol love?

CAROL Eh up. *(Indicating* HARRY *who is counting the seconds off his watch. The two women stand in positions of exaggerated readiness.)*

HARRY Five . . . four . . . three . . . two . . . one! *(Presses switch. Cue machine noises.* MABEL *and* CAROL *go from exaggerated readiness to pantomime of exaggerated chocolate-sorting boredom.* HARRY *checks them, looks at his watch and waits at clocking out machine.)*

MABEL *(After the routine has established itself.)* Mister Chocky's Chocolate Factory.

CAROL Truffle department. *(Enter* ADA, *very late and very anxious. Fumbles at the clocking in.)*

HARRY Ada! You're late again, Ada. *(*ADA *stands motionless, head lowered.)* What did I say would happen to you if you was late again? I said I'd stop your bonus, didn't I, Ada? *(Pause.)* Your bonus is stopped, Ada. *(Pause.)* Now get to bleedin' work. *(*ADA *joins* CAROL *and* MABEL *on the line, avoiding their eyes. She starts sorting.* HARRY *comes up behind.)*

HARRY Know what you are Ada, eh? *(Pause.)* Eh? *(Pause.)* I'll tell you, shall I? *(Pause.)* You're bleedin' 'opeless, that's what you are; and you know what else you are –

MABEL Harry, pet . . . (HARRY *looks at* MABEL.) Sorry to interrupt your little pep-talk, only there's summat I think you ought to know.

HARRY What's that, Mabel love?

MABEL Your flies are undone.

HARRY Bloody Norah! (HARRY *exits, flustered and fiddling with flies.)*

CAROL *(After she stops giggling.)* He'll send you down the road one of these days, you know.

MABEL Nah, not 'Arry. Me an' 'Arry go back a long time. (CAROL *looks enquiringly.)* Never tell you about me an' 'Arry?

CAROL No.

MABEL Used to go out with 'im, didn't I.

CAROL You didn't!

MABEL I did. Years ago, mind you, when 'Arry were a good-lookin' lad an' I were a push-over for owt in trousers with a charmin' smile. Anyhow, it all finished after he got made foreman. Power went straight to 'is head. Rotted 'is looks an' addled 'is brain. *(Pause.)* He asked me to marry 'im.

CAROL He didn't!

MABEL O aye. An' that weren't all he asked me to do, either. Which is why he won't be sending me down the road in an 'urry. I know too much. *(Pause.)* Only picks on Ada 'cos he knows she won't fight back. Rotten sod! All men are sods, love. You learn that.

CAROL I'd rather 'ave 'im, than that 'ard-faced bitch over the typin' pool. Can't stand women bosses.

MABEL Gaffers are gaffers, love – doesn't matter if they pee standin' up or sittin' down. You all right, Ada love? *(*ADA *nods, then pops a chocolate from the line into her mouth.)*

CAROL Eh up, she's off. Truffle snufflin'. Quality control does testin', you know, Ada. *(*ADA *eats another.)* Bloody 'ell, Mabel, she's like an 'oover. What size dress do you take, Ada?

MABEL Leave her alone, she does no harm.

CAROL You 'ave to be cruel to be kind sometimes, Mabel. I mean, how's Ada ever goin' to get herself a fella looking like Cyril Smith in drag? You need to go on a diet, love. Crash diet. Get 'em to wire your teeth together or summat. Lose thirty stone or so an' you might be in with a chance. What did you say love? *(Pause. Then to* MABEL *in mock astonishment.)* She spoke! What were that, Ada? didn't quite catch.

ADA *(After a pause.)* Nuffin'.

CAROL Aww, c'mon, love. It's first bloody thing you've said since you started, so we might as well 'ave the benefit.

MABEL Come on, love, you stick up for yourself. No bugger else will.

ADA *(With difficulty.)* I – I said – I said – fat – fat is a feminin' – feminist . . . somethin'.

CAROL *(*CAROL *exchanges a puzzled glance with* MABEL.*)* What's she goin' on about?

ADA *(With nervous intensity.)* Me social worker, she said it. She says that – that fat is – is a feminist whatsit. I can't remember the other word, but – it means – it means you shouldn't go on diets an' that.

CAROL Bloody 'ell, she *can* talk! What's she on about, though. That's what I want to know?

MABEL *(Kindly.)* Didn't know you 'ad a social worker, love. *(Pause.)* Problems at home, is there?

ADA *(Too emphatically.)* No! No! Nuffin' like that.

MABEL Is she fat, then – this social worker?

ADA Oh no, she's got a lovely figure.

MABEL An' she doesn't diet, or owt?

ADA Oh no. It's bad, see. Even if she was fat herself she wouldn't diet, even then, she says.

MABEL *(Laconically.)* Very principled person, your social worker. *(Enter* DES *furtively.)*

MABEL Eh up, Carol: your randy boyfriend's 'ere.

DES Carol, can you lend us a quid?

CAROL What for?

DES I owe it. *(*CAROL *pulls a face.)* Go on, give it you back when I get me wages.

CAROL Don't know if I've got a quid.

DES Mabel?

MABEL I'm into young fellas, Des – but not that much.

DES Go on, Carol, just 'ave a look in your bag. Quick, before 'Arry sees me. I'm s'posed to be in stores. *(With a long-suffering grimace,* CAROL *looks in her bag.)* You're a good-un, Carol.

CAROL An' you're a bastard.

MABEL Isn't it lovely, young love? Is he always this romantic, Carol?

CAROL Yeah, all the time. There, an' a want it back, right?

DES Thanks, Carol *(Kisses her.)* See you. *(Makes to exit.)*

CAROL Eh, you've not forgot about takin' me to that pub for lunch, 'av you? *(DES stops.)*

DES Er, no. 'Course not.

CAROL You 'ad, 'adn't you! You bleedin' well 'ad! Bloody 'ell, Des, it's only us anniversary today – six months.

DES I know, I know. 'Aven't forgot. It's just . . . *(Pause.)* I've got to put this bet on first, see. So I'll pick you up in the canteen after that, all right? Right. See you! *(Exits, watched by CAROL.)*

MABEL *(Working.)* That's progress, that is. In my day they used to wait till they got married to you before they started treating you like shit. *(Pause.)* Mind you, he's got such a lovely bum you could forgive him anything. *(Fondly remembering.)* My first husband 'ad a bum like 'is. Just like 'is. Chubby little cherub's cheeks that made your hands twitch just to look. I married 'im for 'is bum. *(Getting back to work.)* That an' the fact I were six months gone. What did you say, Ada?

ADA Nuffin'.

CAROL I think she said 'sex objects', but I couldn't swear to it.

MABEL 'Sex objects'? *(Looks at ADA. ADA works on, head down.)* What would you know about sex objects, love?

ADA *(After a pause.)* Me – me social worker, says you shouldn't – shouldn't treat people as – as –

MABEL Sex objects. I'm with you now. Thought you were talkin' about the ones you plug in, love. Got a lot to say for 'erself, this social worker of yours, 'asn't she? *(Carries on working.)* Mind you, they do, don't they, these student types. I know, you see, 'cos me eldest daughter's one.

Except she's not social, she's community. Or is it youth? Anyhow, makes no difference one way or another. They all dress up like builders' mates an' talk crap. Don't know why they call 'emselves workers, 'cos they never seem to do any bleedin' work. Least me daughter doesn't. Just 'as meetin's. An' trainin' courses. Anyhow, Ada pet, these sex objects of yours. What does your social worker say about 'em?

ADA She – she says – that people – shouldn't be treated as them.

CAROL Them?

MABEL Sex objects, love. Men shouldn't treat women as sex objects. An' the other way round, an' all, I s'pose. S'what me daughter says. Problem is, Ada, we are sex objects. All of us. I mean, if we're all just bloody brains in bottles it'd be a poor do, wouldn't it? Nobody ever got an 'ot flush from ogling somebody's brains. Lust. Lust makes the world go round. Love just makes it wobble. I mean, where would we be without lust, eh, Carol? *(*CAROL *shakes her head.)* Extinct – that's where we'd be. Mind you, I'm not sayin' we're *just* sex objects. Just the interestin' bits, that's all. The rude bits. I mean, I've been married to three fellas an' I've 'ad more than you've 'ad 'ot dinners, an' if you piled all their brains in an 'eap an' tried to flog 'em on the market, I wouldn't give you fifty pee for the lot. But there's other bits one or two of 'em I'd pay a lot more for, eh? Like your Desmond's bum, for example, Carol. *(Enter* TREVOR, *pushing a brush.)* Here y'are see, love. Case in point. Trevor. *(No response.)* Trevor, dear.

TREVOR *(Surly.)* What?

MABEL Don't mind people thinkin' you're a sex object, do you!

TREVOR Don't know what you're talkin' about. Give us a chocky truffle. *(Reaches out to grab one.* MABEL *slaps his wrist away.)*

MABEL 'Ands off! You'll get fat and turn into a feminist whatsit and then where would you be?

TREVOR Goin' then. *(Exits.* MABEL *watches him off.)*

MABEL You know, Trevor puts me in mind of this male stripper I saw when I were out on this 'en night a week or two ago. Did I tell you about that, Carol? It were a blindin' night out; all girls together effin' an' blindin' an' tellin' disgustin' jokes, an' this fella comes on stage wearin' nothing but a pair of tartan socks an' this potty over 'is – *(*CAROL *nudges her. Indicates* ADA, *who has her fingers in her ears. Pause. Then, as if talking to a deaf person.)*

MABEL Somethin' wrong, love? *(*ADA *shakes her head.)* Somethin' your social worker said about male strippers? *(*ADA *shakes her head.)* Your mam, then? *(*ADA *shakes her head.)* No? Aww go on, love – I'm dyin' to know.

ADA Sister Theresa. *(*CAROL *and* MABEL *look at each other.)*

MABEL Who, love?

ADA Sister Theresa at school.

MABEL O, I see. You went to a convent school – right? *(*ADA *nods.)* Well, what did Sister Theresa 'ave to say about male strippers, love? Not much, I would 'ave thought.

ADA She said – she said that – that we should never think about anythin' – *(*ADA *looks down.)* – anythin' below. An' when we 'ad a bath, we should float a flannel in front of us in case we looked down by accident. *(Pause.)*

MABEL *(Working.)* Between her social worker an' sister Theresa, poor bugger's not goin' to get much fun out of life, is she? *(Exit* MABEL, ADA *and* CAROL.*)*

SCENE TWO

Cue 'Clever Trevor' by Ian Dury. Enter TREVOR *with a pile of boxes. He looks over his shoulder several times, puts boxes on floor, fiddles for keys, opens a large door, picks boxes up, enters, puts boxes down, closes door, peers out just to check, listens inside door, smiles, sits on one of the boxes and roots through the others till he finds a box of chocolates, eats one, chews happily, roots some more till he finds a copy of* 'The Dandy', *which he raises in front of his face and starts to read. Lowers it suddenly.*

TREVOR Trevor's bailin' shed. *(Presses button. Cue Machine FX. Raises paper back in front of his face. Fade music. Enter* DES *furtively. Stops outside shed. Listens at door, tries to peer through the key hole.)*

DES Trevor?

TREVOR *(Reading.)* 'Korky . . . is . . . in . . . in . . . a . . . fix . . .'

DES You in there, mate?

TREVOR 'Ooh yah!', says Korky, 'Get off my grub!'

DES *(Imitating* HARRY'S *voice.)* 'Trevor – I know you're in there, Trevor, so stop playin' with yourself an' open this bleedin' door.' *(*TREVOR *leaps to feet and scurries about trying to hide his comic and his chocs.)*

TREVOR 'Ang on a mo', 'Arry – just – tidyin' up – just comin' – I'm very sorry, 'Arry, I were. *(Opens door.)* You rotten pig.

DES Thought I were 'Orrible 'Arry – did you Trev? Come for a bit of a rest, mate. *(Pulls out fag.)*

TREVOR Not s'posed to smoke in here. Sign – see?

DES Lots of things you're not s'posed to do in this life, Trev. *(Sits.)* Got a light?

TREVOR *(Sulking.)* No.

DES Aww c'mon, Trevo! You've got everything but the bleedin' kitchen sink in 'ere. Clever Trevor's 'Olesale Bleedin' Warehouse.

TREVOR Don't know what you're talking about.

DES Aye well, you're not as daft as you crack out to be, are you? I mean all the stuff you nick from the factory, Trev. Where've you stashed it? *(Rummages through boxes.)* Aye, aye. What 'ave we 'ere, then? *(Pulls out a box of chocs.)* A one-pound box of Mr Chocky's Chocolate Truffles. Like 'em, do you, Trevor? Naughty but nice, eh? I imagine you'll 'ave bought these, won't you? *(Pops one.)*

TREVOR Yeh, that's right.

DES *(Spits it out.)* Muck. Only fit for givin' to bints when you've forgot birthdays. What else 'ave you got stashed away? *(Rummages. Stops. Looks at* TREVOR.*)* What's this, then? *(Feels.)* You little bleeder. *(Pulls out a handful of* sink plugs on chains.) We've been stuffin' sink 'oles with bog paper for weeks 'cos of you. What you want bloody plugs for?

TREVOR Mind your own business.

DES What else 'ave you got? Bloody Al Capone, you are. *(Pulls out comic.)* This'll be yours, I imagine, Einstein, eh? Didn't think you could read. *(*TREVOR *tries to snatch it off him.)* I'm only lookin', Trevo! *(Flicking through it.)* Well, Trev, this is a cosy little 'ome from 'ome. Better than that bloody council 'ome you live in, anyhow, eh?

TREVOR Don't live there any more.

DES Chuck you out for nickin' sink plugs, did they?

TREVOR Eh? No. Too old, that's all.

DES Bastards, eh. Where you livin' now, then?

TREVOR Flat in Hulme.

DES Well, this'll definitely be cosier than there. Hole in the friggin' skirtin' board'd be cosier than there. *(Throws comic on floor.* TREVOR *scrabbles for it.)* You know, Trevo, you ought to be readin' grown-up stuff at your age. Adult literature. *(Pulls out glossy magazine from overall pocket.)* Wrap your eyeballs round that, sunshine. *(Throws it on the floor in front of Trevor, watches him pick it up with great suspicion and flick through it.)* We've got a club in servicin'. All electricians pay so much a week an' every so often we send one of the YTSs out to the roody shop for the latest skins. *(*TREVOR *is now absorbed, the magazine lifted high in front of his face.)* That one's had several previous owners so don't blame me if the pages are stuck together. Enjoyin' it, are you?

TREVOR *(Lowering the magazine with a glazed look and with the force of profound spiritual revelation.)* Eh, Des. There's women in 'ere – with no clothes on. *(Cue factory whistle.* DES *and* TREVOR *exit.)*

SCENE THREE

MABEL, CAROL *and* ADA *set up chairs together and sit as if at a canteen table.* MABEL *eats;* CAROL *makes herself up;* ADA *reads a book, oblivious to everything.*

MABEL Canteen, dinner hour. *(Lets rip a loud belch.)* I love roly poly puddin'. *(Belches again.)* Trouble is, it doesn't love me.

CAROL Can you see 'im yet, Mabel?

MABEL I wasn't looking. *(Looks.)* No.

CAROL Rotten swine – there's only 'alf an 'our left.

MABEL Look on the bright side, love – that means you've only to spend 'alf an hour with 'im. What's she readin' that's so absorbin'?

CAROL *(Lowers make-up, gently raises* ADA*'s book to look,* ADA *continues to read.)* *Desert Passion*. Mills and Boon.

MABEL Make you blind, them, chuck. *(*ADA *doesn't hear.)*

CAROL What's wrong with 'em? I read 'em all the time when I read owt. Romance and all that. Bit of a laugh, innit? Does no 'arm. I were readin' this one last night. *Forbidden Love*, it were called, an' it were about this trainee nurse who fell in love with this good-lookin' married doctor and she didn't know what to do 'cos this fella really loved her, an' 'is wife wouldn't give him a divorce 'cos she were a right bitch, you know.

MABEL And what happened?

CAROL Oh, it were lovely. This bitch of a wife got run over by a bus an' died. So the nurse could marry the doctor after all – an act of God, like.

MABEL If y'ask me God got wrong one – should have run over the fella.

CAROL Eh up, he's here. *(Jumps up, grabs bag.)* See yous. *(Exits with* DES. MABEL *watches, then shakes head.)*

MABEL How come nobody learns, eh? That's what I want to know. What do you think, pet? Ada? Ada, love? (ADA *pops choc, still reading.)* Yoo hoo, this is ground control, Ada. Are you receiving me?

ADA Eh? Oh, I were . . . *(Shows book.)*

MABEL Like them books, do you, love? (ADA *nods.)* Read a lot of 'em, do you? (ADA *nods.)* Get them off your mam, do you? (ADA *nods.)* Get on with your mam, do you? (ADA *nods)* What's she like, your mam?

ADA *(Encouraged by Mabel's gentle persistance.)* She's – she's little. Wi' – wi' brown hair – an' a sort of white face. Quiet.

MABEL Like you? (ADA *nods.)* An' what's your dad like? (ADA *lowers head.)* 'Ave you got a dad? (ADA *nods.)* But you don't like to talk about 'im? (ADA *remains still.)* Live with your mam, does he? (ADA *nods.)* Is he why you've got a social worker? (ADA *nods.)* Bet he's not quiet, is he? (ADA *shakes head.)* Not much of a conversationalist, are you, love? (MABEL *gets fag out.)* What do you and your mam do for fun – I mean when your dad's out boozin' – I presume he's a boozer? (ADA *nods.)* What do you do when he's out?

ADA Housework.

MABEL I mean, after your housework's done.

ADA We – we – we just sit and – be quiet.

MABEL What about lads, love? (ADA *looks embarrassed.)* Not got a boyfriend yet? Wouldn't worry too much about that, chuck, there's plenty of time yet. I mean, you want to take no notice of Carol. I mean, she's a good lass but she's lad mad. Thinks you have to look like Madonna to get 'em.

She'll learn. Makes no odds what you look like in the end. It's personality that counts. *(Lights fag.)* Anyhow, you're better off with a late start, if y'ask me. They're like cigarettes, men. *(Takes deep drag.)* Once you've started, it's bloody difficult to stop and they do you no bloody good in the end. *(Takes another drag.)* I should know. Married three of 'em, didn't I? Give me four kids – all grown up now, of course, an' I got rid of me last husband last year. An' I've never felt better. *(MABEL is absorbed in her thoughts. ADA watches her with a puzzled expression and eventually returns to her book.)* Great it is. Do what I want when I want. Go out when I want, come in when I want. Do the tidyin' up when I want, don't if I don't want, watch what I want on the video without 'avin' to put up with bloody John Wayne or Clint Eastwood every night or 'is daft blue films. Go to bed with me warm woolly socks on, a cup of hot milk an' a raw onion butty. On me own. No bugger stickin' 'is bony knees into me back, stealin' all me sheets an' snorin' like a bloody elephant in labour. *(Pause.)* An' nobody farts but me. Mind you, I still get the odd twinge now and again. Withdrawal symptoms, I think they call it. Or maybe it's just loneliness. Not that I 'aven't got lots of women friends, it's just – an' then some middle-aged bugger with a Bobby Charlton haircut asks you out and gets you a drink an' treats you with a bit of consideration and that sets you off with your daft half-pissed thoughts about Mister Right and all that bloody nonsense. You never grow up in some ways. Anyhow, then you sober up and see 'im again and get to know him and that usually does the trick – he starts askin' you to sew buttons on his shirt and you realise in a flash what it is you're not missin' and you show 'im the door, thank you very much but not today thank you. *(She notices ADA.)* You've not heard a bloody word I've been sayin', 'ave you, love? Mind you, why should you? It's natural, innit, to make bloody fools of ourselves. If you're a lass you're after lads, an' if you're a lad you're after lasses, an' it's rough if you don't look like what the bloody hair, make-up and frock people say you should look like. Where would we be if everybody thought like me, eh? You don't get babies eatin' raw onion butties, do you? *(*HARRY *enters, hovers nervously to rear.)* No, love, get stuck in. Everybody wants to be wanted, love. I mean, I dare say your mam loves you, doesn't she? But that's not enough, is it? You want to be loved by a stranger, for what y'are. *(Pause.)* Or what they think y'are. Or what they think they can get out of you. You want it, whether or not, an' you keep on wantin' it no matter what 'appens or what you tell yourself. You want it even if they treat you like a dish rag for ever after. *(Factory whistle goes.)*

HARRY Ada! (ADA *jumps.)* Get to work. (ADA *scurries off.* MABEL *takes her time.)*

MABEL You used to be such a nice lad, an' all.

HARRY Aye – aye – well. This is work. Work's work.

MABEL *(Exiting.)* You missed your way, 'Arry – should 'ave been a philosopher.

HARRY Mabel! (MABEL *stops.)* I mean – I'd – I'd like a bit of a word, if you don't mind, love.

Scene Four

Loud pub music. Des playing darts with an invisible partner. CAROL *sits, knees together, bag on knee, eating something out of a packet and looking pig-sick.*

DES Treble nine. *(Pulling darts out of board.)* Eleven, double six makes twelve and treble nine makes fifty. You're knackered, mate. Go on. *(Watches as, we assume, his mate starts to throw.)*

CAROL Des.

DES *(Watching the board.)* Yeah? *(To mate.)* Hah! Try 'ittin' the board.

CAROL Des!

DES What?

CAROL You said you were goin' to buy me lunch here.

DES I just did, didn't I? *(To mate.)* Fifteen! You're out of your class, mate! Now get out of the road an' let the expert 'ave a go. *(Starts to aim.)*

CAROL *(Indicating packet.)* This isn't lunch.

DES *(Throwing dart.)* You said you were slimmin'.

CAROL I said slimmin' – not goin' on friggin' hunger strike.

DES *(Pauses in mid-aim.)* 'Ang on a minute, Dave, will you? Women trouble. *(Goes over to* CAROL.*)* Look – if you don't want 'em, give 'em 'ere. *(Grabs packet and stuffs handful of contents in his mouth.)* I love pork cracklin'.

CAROL Least you could do is get me another drink.

DES After I've finished pastin' this wimp. *(To mate.)* Double three'll do it. *(Throws.)* What did I tell you! Magic – sheer bloody magic! I'll give you a chance for revenge tomorrow, all right? Got to see the wife before she gets 'er rollin' pin out. *(To* CAROL.*)* You want a drink? *(Goes to bar.)* Britvik orange, love, an' another pint of Boddies. *(Waits, looks at* CAROL, *smiles.* CAROL *pulls a face.* DES *raises eyebrows to barmaid.)* Women, eh? How much, love? *(Looks in pockets.)* Shit! Eh, er, Carol, love. 'Aven't got any change, have you? That bet I put on – it lost – horse 'ad been got at – died. *(*CAROL *angrily hands over money from her bag.)* Ta. *(Brings drinks over. Sits next to* CAROL. *Smiles.* CAROL *stares in front. Long pause.)* Well, this is nice, innit? *(Silence.)* What's been 'appenin' to you, then, love? *(Pause.)* Aww, come on, Carol – don't let's not speak – I mean – it's us anniversary, isn't it! Six months since we started – since I first saw you sortin' truffles an' fell in love right off. *(Pause.)* Head over heels. *(Pause.)* Come on, tell us somethin'.

CAROL *(Reluctantly.)* Ada said summat.

DES That fat bint? Thought she were deaf and dumb.

CAROL So did we. I were takin' the micky out of 'er, you know. For a bit of a laugh. Feel guilty about it now. She's – she's sort of pathetic. Feel sorry for 'er. I don't think she's ever 'ad a boyfriend or anythin'.

DES Not surprised. *(To someone who has just entered.)* Phil! Goin' to the match on Saturday? Yah! Part-time supporter!

CAROL Des!

DES What!

CAROL I think she needs a boyfriend. Do you know anybody who'd – you know – take her out?

DES *(Choking on his beer.)* You're jokin'! 'Ave to be blind. Or daft. I don't know anybody daft enough. *(Cue suddenly 'Clever Trevor'.)* 'Ang on a minute, I do. I do know somebody daft enough. Daft enough for owt. Eh, what a laugh, eh, Carol? Clever Trevor. Clever Trevor an' 'orrible Ada. Great loves of our time. Look – this is what we do, right? What we do is . . .

SCENE FIVE

DES *crosses to Trevor, who is on his box reading the porno mag.* DES *hangs around behind him for a few seconds.*

DES Ever been out with a girl, Trev?

TREVOR *(Still reading.)* 'Course I 'ave.

DES How many?

TREVOR 'Undreds.

DES You don't 'ave to lie to me, Trev. I'm your mate, right? 'Ow many, Trev – really?

TREVOR I told you – loads.

DES Know what 'appens to lads who tell lies about their sex lives, Trevo?

TREVOR No.

DES Their plonker drops off.

TREVOR *(Lowering magazine, frowns.)* You're 'avin' me on.

DES Honest to God, Trev, It's a medical fact. Saw this documentary on Channel Four. So tell the truth, Trev, to your old mate. How many? Three? *(Pause.* TREV *shakes head.)* Two? *(*TREV *shakes head.)* One? *(Longer pause.* TREV *makes to nod, then shakes head again.)* Not as many as one, eh? Dear me, Trevor, how old are you?

TREVOR Eighteen and three quarters.

DES Know 'ow many women I'd 'ad by the time I were your age, Trev? *(*TREVOR *shakes his head.* DES *wheedles in his ear.)* A lot, Trevor. I'd 'ad two kids by the time I were sixteen, mate. So you've a lot of catchin' up to do if – you know – if you want to be a real man, Trevor. *(Insistent, in* TREV*'s ear.)* You do, don't you – want to be a real man.

TREVOR Yeah, yeah, 'course, Des. But –

DES I know somebody who fancies you, Trevo!

TREVOR Me? Who?

DES She's dead fit, Trev. Fleshy.

TREVOR Who is it?

DES Ada on chocolate truffles.

TREVOR Ugh – she's fow.

DES She's got a very pleasant personality, Trev.

TREVOR She's fat.

DES You don't look at the mantelpiece when you're stokin' fire, do you, Trev?

TREVOR What you mean?

DES These fow women – they're real goers on the sly. Got to be, 'aven't they? Only way they can get fellas, isn't it?

TREVOR Goers?

DES Bleedin' 'ell, Trev – do you want a diagram?

TREVOR Diagram? What of, Des?

DES *(Trying to be patient.)* She'll let you – do things. You know – with 'er body. *(Pause – not getting through.)* Like the women in the book, Trevor.

TREVOR *(Refers to book, studies a page.)* Things like this, Des?

DES *(Looking.)* Er – sort of. That kind of thing, anyhow, mate.

TREVOR An' what would I 'ave to do, Des?

DES Jesus, Trevor, didn't they 'ave sex education at your school?

TREVOR Oh yeah, yeah. *(Pause.)* I think so. RE teacher passed these balloons round for us to look at and then he talked about bees and asked us if we 'ad any questions. None of us 'ad. It were borin'.

DES See your problem, Trev. Right. Well, you can't go round in this dismal ignorance all your life now, can you? Well, this is it then, Trev. Your sex education starts here.

SCENE SIX

Machine FX or music. CAROL. ADA *on line*

CAROL Ada. Ever been out with a lad? *(*MABEL *glances at* CAROL. ADA *stops working momentarily, then lowers head and carries on.)* Thought so. Would you like to?

MABEL Carol . . .

CAROL S'all right, Mabel, I'm not takin' the mickey or owt. *(Pause.)* Would you like to, Ada? *(*ADA *pops a choc, head still down.)* You see – I know one who fancies you. *(*ADA *stops working, head still down.)* A dead lot. *(*ADA *looks at* CAROL *out of the corner of her eye.)* Eh, an' you want to see 'im, an' all. He's – he's dead romantic. Looks like – like that Arabian sheik on the cover of that book you were readin'. *(Freeze.)*

DES Right – ready, Trev? Imagine I'm Ada – get up. *(*TREV *stands,* DES *sits down as girl.)* I'm Ada, right, and you're goin' to ask me out, right? For the first time. Right. Ask me out. *(Pause.)* Go on. *(Pause.)* Come on, you slow bugger, get crackin'. Say, 'Ada'.

TREVOR Ada.

DES *(In falsetto.)* Yes, Trevor.

TREVOR *(Thinks hard, then:)* Will you let me do things to your body like in this book? *(Freeze.)*

CAROL You want to go out with 'im, right? So what do you do? *(*ADA *stares downwards, still.)* Well, what you don't do is go up to him and say, 'Will you come out with me', do you! 'Cos lads don't like that 'cos they like to think they're in control, an' in any case, if you do that he'll think you're too easy an' then you've got all sorts of problems. So what you do is try to attract his attention. You look at 'im across a crowded room, try an' catch 'is eye, see? Then you look away quick, like you weren't tryin' to catch it at all. An' then you try to catch it again. An' after a day or two he's probably got the idea an' you can give him a little smile – like this. *(Smiles.)* Mona Lisa smile. And then he comes and asks you out. *(Pause.)* Got it? Right – let's start wi' catching his eye. I'm this dishy lad, right? *(Acts part, combs hair, swaggers, etc.)* An' you're you. Now, catch me eye. Go on, 'ave a go. *(Long pause.* ADA *embarrassed, then slowly, she winks one eye, and then the other.)* Right, try again shall we, love? *(Freeze.)*

DES *(Crossing to* ADA, MABEL, *and* CAROL, *who remain frozen, except as indicated.)* You go up to her an' you say summat dead smooth like, 'Want to come to the pictures with me, darlin'?', or, 'I've got two tickets for Belle-Vue Speedway, do you fancy comin' with me?' and then she says . . .

CAROL *(To Des.)* 'Sorry, love, I'm washin' me 'air tonight.' *(*DES *turns back on her.)* 'Cos you don't want to show too interested at first, do you? And then he says . . . *(Freeze.)*

DES *(To* ADA.) 'How about some other night, then.' 'Cos, you know she's only playin' 'ard to get. They like to be 'unted, see – flatters 'em.

CAROL *(To* ADA, *but also at* DES *– the dialogue should be played as an aggro match between* CAROL *and* DES, *as much as those two advising* ADA *and* TREV.) And maybe after a bit you say yes – if you want. But not like you're keen, or owt. You say, 'All right, then – I don't mind if I do' like you could take it or leave it. 'Cos fellas only want what they 'aven't got, so it's best to keep 'em on tenterhooks.

DES So you're all fixed up, an' you feel great. You've got a girlfriend.

CAROL You've got a lad, you're walkin' on air.

DES But you've got to keep a grip 'cos the most difficult bit's got to come.

CAROL Like there's your clothes an 'air to be planned. *(Freeze.)*

DES You've got to dress right, right? Now, what do you wear, Trev, when you're goin' out on the razzle.

TREVOR Never been on a razzle.

DES What do you wear for best?

TREVOR Got a jacket.

DES What kind of jacket, Trev?

TREVOR Sports jacket – sort of 'airy, an' I've got some shoes.

DES Yeh, well you need 'em in this cold weather, don't you. What they like, Trev?!

TREVOR Sort of reddy brown they are, with elastic sides an' little holes in the pattern all over the top.

DES Stick to your work clothes, I would, Trev. *(Freeze.)*

CAROL Make-up. You don't want to be goin' out lookin' like you've been dug up, do you? You've got to look like whoever's got her face on magazine covers, right? It's sultry just now, so you puts lots of liner an' mascara on, an' stuff under your cheek bones, right? For example, you've got too much rouge on your cheeks at the moment, Ada.

ADA I'm not wearin' rouge. *(Freeze.)*

DES An' y'ave a bath. Important that. All over. Lots of soap, Trev, got that? An' wash your 'air, an' all. *(Feels* TREV's *hair.)* Not in the chip pan, Trev, right? An' you talc yourself in all your cracks, shoot some Brut up your armpits an' give your mop a good combin'. Got a comb, have you, Trev? *(*TREV *shakes head.)* You can borrow mine. You use two mirrors, an' all. That's so you can see yourself side on. Then you give your nose a good pickin' and out you go. *(Pause.)* Oh aye, Trev. *(Slowly.)* You don't forget to put your clothes on before you leave the 'ouse. *(Freeze.)*

CAROL *(Staring at* DES.) You meet, right? And you'll 'ave to talk, won't you? Now listen. Don't talk too much or say anythin' too clever. 'Cos they don't like brainy women, 'cos it makes 'em realise how thick they are. Better just to listen to 'em – it's borin' for you, but they like it a lot. *(Freeze.)*

DES Chat. You'll 'ave to do most of it! It's bloody borin' but they expect it and you can't start off gropin' right away, can you? Not unless you're dead lucky. So you tell 'em about somethin' thrillin' that you do. *(Looks at* TREV.*)* Ever do anythin' thrillin', Trevor? *(Pause.)* Make summat up. Tell 'er you're a champion 'ang glider, or you wrestle piranhas at weekends. An' notice what they're wearin'? You don't 'ave to do that when you've been goin' out with'em for a bit but it's essential for starters. So: chat, chat, bla, bla, bla, till it's gettin' on a bit an' it's time for what you're really after . . .

CAROL Sex. Now listen carefully, love, this is important. You don't let 'im 'ave a soddin' thing, right? 'Cos if you do he'll think your cheap and tell 'is mates about you next day, makin' up all sorts of stuff you never did just to make 'im look good. No – what you've got to do is . . .

DES *(Walking round* CAROL.) Get 'em worked up. Start with their sensitive bits. Woman 'ave different sensitive bits than men. Necks, for example. Necks is very sensitive on bints. An' earlobes. Nibble their earlobes. *(Crossing back to* TREV.*)* Earlobes, Trev. *(Grabs* TREV*'s earlobes.)* That's an earlobe, Trev, right? That's what you nibble. Leave the bits that you're after till later. *(Watches* CAROL.*)*

CAROL The most you should let 'im 'ave first time round is let him have a fiddle of your tits through your bra. After that, you pull 'is 'and out and tell him what a wonderful time you've 'ad but it's time you were gettin' 'ome to your sick mother, thank you very much.

DES If that doesn't work, start talkin' nice. *(Walking round* CAROL.*)* About how you've not felt like this about anybody before an' all that crap. But if you're still not gettin' what you want, an' you've been goin' out with 'er for ages –

TREVOR How long, Des?

DES A week. Then you're probably either goin' to 'ave to finish with 'er or tell 'er you love 'er, but that's a dodgy trick, is that. Only for real emergencies. 'Cos you never know where it can lead to. She'll 'ave you washin' shitty nappies before you can say, 'I don't', to the vicar. *(Watches* CAROL.*)*

CAROL Now listen, Ada, if he starts sayin' he loves you, you've got to be very careful, 'cos it either means he loves you or he doesn't love you at all but he can't think of any other way of gettin' 'is evil way. *(This is directed at* DES.*)* And that's when you fly solo, love. 'Cos only you can decide that one. Right, Mabel?

MABEL I'm keepin' out of this one, love. I'm too old to say owt you'd want to listen to.

CAROL If you decide he's tellin' the truth, then you can go all the way – if you want. But you don't let 'im do owt you don't want, right? No matter what crap he comes out with. 'Cos it's your body, not 'is. An' if he starts gettin' rough or owt, you just knee him in the knackers an' run 'ome. 'Ave you got that, love?

DES 'Ave you got all that, Trev?

TREVOR Yeah, sure.

DES Right, mate. This is it. Into the chocolate truffle department. *(They cross to the line.)*

CAROL He's 'ere, Ada. I told you, didn't I?

ADA 'Im? He's 'orrible.

CAROL He's got hidden depths, Ada. Now just remember what I said.

MABEL I hope you know what you're doin', lady.

CAROL 'Course I do. Ada's got to start livin' some time, 'asn't she? *(*DES *pushes* TREV *forward, exchanging winks with* CAROL.*)*

DES Go on then, Trev.

TREVOR *(After a lot of false starts.)* Hello. *(Looks back at* DES *helplessly.* DES *urges him on.)* Tr . . . er. *(Pause.)* Would you . . . I want . . . I'd like . . . I'd really like . . . *(He has been fingering the magazine nervously. He now grasps at it last-straw-wise blurting:)* I want you to do what these women in 'ere do! *(Pause.)* Please! *(*CAROL *and* DES *cover their eyes with their hands. Blackout.)*

SCENE SEVEN

Night. ADA, *dressed up in something ghastly, stands as if waiting outside somewhere. Enter* CAROL, *looking good.*

CAROL Hello, love, been 'ere long?

ADA Bit.

CAROL Didn't think you'd turn up. It'll be all right, this, don't worry. With me an' Des there. Easier, innit? It's perishin'. You should 'ave gone in.

ADA Didn't like.

CAROL It's all right, this pub. Me an' Des go in regular, so they know I'm taken an' nobody bothers you even if you're on your own. There's not many pubs I'd sit in on me own though. Too many married men gropin' round you and breathin' dog's breath and Boddies in your face. Come on in, anyhow. Bet Des and Trev are already there. *(Exit. Blackout. Cue pub music.)*

SCENE EIGHT

TREV *and* DES *miming game of pool.* CAROL *and* ADA *sitting side by side, bags on knees, looking bored.*

DES In the Dog an' Duck.

CAROL Hours later. *(*TREVOR *is painstakingly trying to line up a shot.* DES *looking on with exasperation.)*

DES Other way round, Trev. *(*TREV *tries to play the shot backwards.)* The cue, Trev, the cue.

TREVOR Oh, right. *(Turns cue right way up. Lines up shot, tongue between teeth. Makes it. Both watch it bounce backwards and forwards for a ludicrously long time, then it drops in the pocket.* TREV *is over the moon.)* I potted black, Des! Black, Des, potted it. *(Retrieves the potted black and holds it up.)* Black Des.

DES Great, Trev. Only thing is you've not put owt else down yet. I just won.

TREVOR *(Following* DES *back to the women.)* Don't get that, Des.

DES Never mind, Trevor, it were only the fifth game tonight. Maybe after a few 'undred more, eh? Go an' get us another pint for after this, will you, an' two more rum an' blacks for the women. *(*TREV *goes to the bar.* DES *sits next to* CAROL, *who is tightlipped. Silence.)* Been a smashin' evenin', 'asn't it? *(Pause.)* Beat Trev at five games of pool, seven of darts, three of dominoes an' two of pushpenny. Must of poured seven pints of bitter down me neck, not countin' that Drambui that old bid left behind 'er, got me jaws round three meat pies, four packets of prawn cocktail crisps, packet of pork cracklin', Mars bar, an' a pot of mussels. *(Leaning over, face to face with* ADA.*)* That's high livin' for you, eh? *(*ADA *looks disgusted, pulls* *away.)* I mean, you feel like lettin' off a bit of steam after a week at Chocky's, eh? You girls all right, are we? Been talkin' girls' talk, 'ave you? *(Silence.)* Make-up an' clothes an' lads an' menstruation an' that? *(Silence. Leans over to* ADA *again.)* Goin' to the bog in two's, eh! *(*ADA *shifts to the very edge of her seat.)* Please yourself. *(*DES *begins to have problems with the contents of his stomach.)* I think. I think I'm goin' to throw up. *(Runs to front and freezes in mid-vomit.)*

TREVOR Last orders went ten minutes ago, Des, she says. *(Sound of* DES *vomiting.)*

Scene Nine

DES *continues vomiting, bent over at front of stage.* CAROL *stands behind him.* ADA *and* TREV *watch from shadows at the back.*

CAROL *(Angry, upset, nearly in tears.)* I've 'ad it up to 'ere with you! You gamble, you booze, you doss off work, you treat me like I was shit. Are you listenin' to me, you pig? *(*DES *vomits again.* MABEL *enters during the next speech, notices and stops to listen at rear.)* I thought – I thought we 'ad somethin', you an' me, I thought we were goin' to make somethin' together, I thought one of these days we'd *(*DES *vomits.* CAROL *turns away in anger and frustration.)*

MABEL 'Avin' a bit of trouble, love?

CAROL No. Yes. It's him. It's men. It's everythin' – I've 'ad enough. I've watched me mam all her life livin' with a fella like that an' I said I'd never end up like that meself and look at me. Look at him. *(*DES *vomits.)* Mabel. *(Goes into* MABEL*'s arms.)* What am I goin' to do, it's bloody stupid, I hate 'im but I love 'im as well.

MABEL Yeh, I know. I know, love.

CAROL What am I goin' to do, he's all I've got.

MABEL That's daft talk. You're only a lass, you've got a job, you're your own boss.

CAROL Job's crap. I 'ate me job.

MABEL It's a job though, isn't it! Your own money. You don't need 'is. An' you're not tied with kids yet either. Look, come with me an' 'ave a drink, tell me all your troubles an' I'll tell you mine.

CAROL *(Pulling herself together.)* No, thanks, but I'm too fed up. I'd only make you miserable too. I'll go home.

MABEL Up to you love. All right – I'll see you tomorrow, all right? *(Walking to rear. Stops.)* Eh, don't let the bastards get you down, eh?

CAROL No. Yeh. Thanks. See you. *(Exit* MABEL. CAROL *composes herself with a lot of tissue work whilst* DES *coughs up the last bits.)* I'm goin' now, you bastard. Goin' home. We're finished. Right. Finished. An' don't think you can wheedle round me 'cos you can't. I've 'ad enough of you. So goodbye and good riddance. *(Makes for exit.)*

DES *(Looking between his legs at the audience.)* Carol? *(Stands up.)* Carol! *(Runs after her, grabs her.)* Carol – I'm sorry.

CAROL So what – *(Pulls away.)*

DES *(Grabbing her again.)* Carol . . .

CAROL *(Shouting.)* Get off me, you drunken pig, or I'll scream!

DES *(Stepping back, hands in the air.)* All right, all right, I'm off you. Now are you goin' to listen or not?

CAROL Why should I?

DES 'Cos I'm askin' you to. Please.

CAROL Get stuffed. *(Turns, takes a step or two away, stops, turns back.)* What do you think I am, eh? What? Nowt? Shit? I'm a person, right – see? I don't need you, I can live without you. 'Ave you seen me mam? What she's like? Eh, 'ave you? Well, I'm not goin' to be like 'er. I'm not wastin' me life on a bloody fella – fetchin' an' carryin' and puttin' up with your soddin' vomit of a Saturday night – I'm buggered if I'm doin' that – so you can piss off for me – you can piss off! *(Turns, steps away.)*

DES *(Panic.)* Carol! *(*CAROL *stops, takes another step away.* DES *is desperate.)* Carol, for Christ's sake! *(*CAROL *stops again.)* Don't. Don't. I love you. I do. *(*CAROL *turns,* *caught by his tone of voice.)* I – I don't want to lose you. *(Glances at* ADA *and* TREVOR *in shadows, lowers voice.)* I mean that.

CAROL You just want to get me knickers off.

DES No I don't. I mean, I do. But that's not why I'm sayin' it. I can't do without you. Just now when you said you'd finished with me – it felt – it felt like – like you'd ripped half me insides out just sayin' it. Like there was this bleedin' great black hole inside myself that I were fallin' into. I'm no good without you, Carol. I'm – I'm just nothin' – talk – bullshit – there's nothin' inside me. Do you believe me?

CAROL I don't know. I know you too well.

DES *(Pressing his advantage.)* Can I walk you home?

CAROL I'm goin' 'ome. I can't stop you walkin' the same way if you want. *(*DES *scurries over to her. She links arms with him.* CAROL *glances at* TREVOR *and* ADA.*)* Me mam were a mug an' all. *(*CAROL *and* DES *exit.)*

SCENE TEN

TREVOR *and* ADA *stand awkwardly. Music.* TREVOR *gestures* ADA *to sit. She stares at him, then does so. Then pops a choc.* TREVOR *sits nervously next to her. Pause. After several false starts* TREVOR *thrusts his mouth at the side of* ADA*'s head. She screams and leaps away.* TREVOR *leaps up in shock at this reaction.*

TREVOR Sorry, I were –

ADA What do you think you were doin'?

TREVOR I thought –

ADA You thought what?

TREVOR I thought you were supposed to like it.

ADA What are you talkin' about?

TREVOR 'Avin' your ear nibbled.

ADA *(Rubbing side of head.)* You're mad. You nearly bit it off.

TREVOR I'm sorry. I didn't – I didn't – didn't mean –

ADA *(With surprising vehemence.)* Shut up! (TREVOR *shuts up.* ADA *stares at him, pops a choc, chews it, then sits down again.)* You look stupid standing there. Sit down! (TREVOR *obediently sits.* ADA *looks at him.)* You don't look a bit like a sheik.

TREVOR Eh?

ADA Be quiet. *(She pops another choc.)* Stupid – you're so stupid. Everybody. *(Chews, pause.)* Just 'cos I don't say much you think I'm stupid – but I'm not. Don't know who's more stupid, men or women. Men – braggin' an' fighting an' killin' an' tryin' to be better than each other all the time. Always tryin' to put their little thingies into women. That's what you want to do with me, isn't it? (TREVOR *looks down.*) Isn't it?! I know. You don't 'ave to be clever to do that, you know. There's nothing to it. Seen my gerbils do it. I've 'eard me mam an' dad. When he's not drunk. Or 'ittin' her. Or 'ittin' me, or 'ittin' the dog, or 'ittin' the wall. But you're not doin' it with me now, so don't think y'are. Women. Me mam. Her, Carol. Moanin' an' moanin' all the time and comin' back for more. Puttin' up with it. They must like it or else they wouldn't, would they? Even me social worker. Goin' on. But she told me the other day it's always 'er who does the 'ousework an' washin' an' that, so what's she goin' on about? Hot air. It's 'cos she wants a baby. That's what it is. You can't have babies without men. *(Looks at* TREVOR.*)* You did know that? Well, I don't want one, so I don't need you. So there. Don't need anybody, me. Once you start, needin' people, they muck you up. *(Pops choc.)* I'm goin' now. *(Walks away.* TREVOR *thinks, then stands suddenly.)*

TREVOR Eh! (ADA *turns.*)

ADA What?

TREVOR Can I walk you home?

ADA No. *(Turns, takes two steps, stops. Turns back.)* What do you want to walk me 'ome for?

TREVOR I like you.

ADA You're stupid. *(Turns. Takes two steps. Stops. Thinks. Turns round slowly. Pause.)* Do you really?

TREVOR I've never met anybody like you before.

ADA Des told you to say that.

TREVOR He didn't! *(Pause.)* He did. (ADA *turns away.)* But I mean it! (ADA *stops.)* I've never met anybody as – as brainy as you. You say – brainy things. I mean – I've never – never 'ad a mam or dad or owt – I mean – I – I know I'm thick – not brainy – but I can't 'elp that an' I'm good at – they taught me loads of things at the 'ome. Like – I can do errands an' – an' sweep up. Will you say summat brainy again? – I like it – summat like you said before – anythin'. *(*ADA *stares at him, then slowly approaches. Holds his face in both hands and pecks him on the lips, and then stands back.)*

ADA That were a kiss. Tara. *(Exits.)*

TREVOR *(Hand on mouth as if to verify.)* Eh! I will walk you 'ome. *(Exits.)*

SCENE ELEVEN

Factory whistle continues. Enter CAROL *and* MABEL. MABEL *is flustered.*

CAROL Mornin', Mabel.

MABEL Mornin'. Overslept.

CAROL *(Clocking in.)* Not like you that.

MABEL Aye – well I 'ad a bit of a night of it.

CAROL It's the raw onion butties that do that. *(Settling in on line.)* Eh – you weren't meetin' a fella in that pub, were you?

MABEL Might 'ave.

CAROL Was he all right?

MABEL All right under the circumstances: he was a fella.

CAROL How old?

MABEL Too old, like me.

CAROL You fancy 'im though, don't you, I can tell!

MABEL I might.

CAROL Oh Mabel, I'm dead pleased for you. *(Hugs her. Enter* DES.*)*

DES Aye aye, what's this then?

MABEL Female solidarity, Des, on account of us both being soddin' stupid.

DES Oh. Right then. I'm off to the shed for me pre-work tea-break. See you in the pub at dinner, Carol.

CAROL Yeh, s'pose so.

DES Yeh. Great. Great. *(Exits.)*

MABEL You didn't 'ave 'im back, did you? (CAROL *nods.*) Shi-i . . .there's no hope for us, is there!

CAROL Eh up, Harry's here. He's late, never seen him late, have you, Mabel.

MABEL No. No. I haven't. (ADA *comes in behind Harry.*)

HARRY Ada. (ADA *stops.*) You're late again, Ada. (ADA *lowers head.*) What did I say would happen to you if you was late again?

MABEL Harry!

HARRY I'll tell you what I said – I said –

MABEL Harold!

HARRY Eh?

MABEL There's somethin' I think y'ought to know.

HARRY A-ah! You can't pull that one on me again, Mabel. These are new trousers, these are. Zip don't slip down, see!

MABEL I wasn't goin' to say anythin' about your flies, Harold.

HARRY What then? (MABEL *stares at him knowingly.* CAROL *looks from one to the other.*) That's blackmail, Mabel.

MABEL Isn't it just.

HARRY You're an 'ard woman, Mabel.

MABEL Oh, I don't know Harry. I 'ave me soft bits. (*Exit Harry.*) See you tonight, eh, chuck!? Oh aye, (*Shouting after.*) an' wear your old trousers, all right?

CAROL Mabel.

MABEL There's an old sayin': better the devil you know than one you don't. Harry's not so bad. He's been very lonely since 'is wife died. (*Freeze. Cue 'Clever Trevor'. Enter* TREVOR *with boxes. Looks over shoulder. Puts boxes down.*

Fiddles with keys. Opens door. Picks boxes up, enters, sits on box. Roots around. Pops choc. Holds up Dandy *and* Porno *as if deciding which to read. Chooses* Dandy. *Presses button. Cue machine noises. Enter* DES *as before. Peeps through door jamb.)*

DES Trevor? *(No response. In* HARRY'*s voice.)* Trevor, I know what you're doin' in there and you'd better stop it or I'll call the police.

TREVOR *(Leaping up and scurrying about.)* Sorry, 'Arry! I were – I were only – just – *(Opens door.)* You rotten bastard!

DES *(Entering.)* Never fails, does it, Trev? Got a light?

TREVOR *(Sulking.)* No. *(*DES *roots about in the box. Pulls out handful of plugs, shakes head, puts them back. Picks up porno mag, opens it, then to* TREV.*)*

DES Eh – how'd you get on with sexy Ada last night, Trev?

TREVOR *(Defensive.)* All right.

DES *(Approaching.)* Give 'er one, did you?

TREVOR Give 'er one what Des? *(Freeze.)*

CAROL How were it with Trev after I left, Ada?

ADA *(After a pause.)* All right.

CAROL Were it like in your Mills and Boon, then? All romantic and lovely? *(Freeze.)*

DES Did you get her goin'? Like I said: ears and neck and then movin' down?

TREVOR (After a pause.) Might 'ave. *(Freeze.)*

CAROL Did he say he'd never met anybody like you before in 'is whole life? Eh – did he say that?

ADA *(After a pause.)* He might have. *(Freeze.)*

DES Did she let you 'ave it, Trev? All the way – number ten?

CAROL Did he say he loves you, Ada, eh? *(*TREVOR *looks across at Ada, Ada looks across at* TREVOR.*)*

DES Did she, Trev?

CAROL Did he, Ada? *(Long pause.* TREVOR *and* ADA *look away from each other.)*

TREVOR Er – er, yeh. Yeh, she did. She did, Des.

ADA Yeh – he did. He did, Carol.

DES Bloody great, mate. *(Holding porno mag.)* Join the club! We'll make a man out of you yet.

CAROL Aww, isn't that nice. Isn't that nice, Mabel. Just like in her books. Isn't it lovely, eh? *(All freeze, except* MABEL.*)*

MABEL Yeh. Isn't it. Isn't it just.

Trappin'

Frances McNeil

Cast

VIV

JANE

GARRY

LAURIE

MRS BENSON (VIV'S MUM)

DOCTOR

First performed by M6 Theatre Company, Rochdale.

'*Trappin*'' is Rochdale slang for getting a boyfriend or girlfriend.

SCENE ONE

Flat – an evening in September, Year 1.
VIV, *still wearing her office clothes, emerges from the kitchen, carrying a cup of tea. Her suit jacket is on the sofa and the bag she takes to work is by her shoes on the floor. She takes her folded copy of* Cosmo *from the bag, perches her cup precariously and sprawls on the sofa – reading* Cosmo.

The doorbell rings. VIV *checks her watch, frowns, straightens the scatter cushions and bounces across the room into the hall.*

VIV *(Speaking into intercom.)* Garry?

JANE Viv, it's me, Jane.

VIV Jane! Come up.

VIV *presses button to release door. She waits, smiles to herself, and counts the seconds. After five seconds, the bell rings again.*

VIV Jane?

JANE How do I get in?

VIV Push the door on the buzz – dumbo! *(Pressing button.)* Push!

The phone rings. VIV *doesn't answer it but picks up her suit jacket from the sofa and takes it through to the bedroom. Then she goes to the door and lets* JANE *in.*

VIV Hiya!

JANE Hey, you look great.

VIV You do too.

JANE I hate to say it, but he obviously agrees with you.

VIV Just a bit. Park your bum.

JANE It's looking very swish in here.

VIV We like it.

JANE I can see it all: lots of entertaining, dinner for Garry's boss and all that. No time for your old mates.

VIV I've been meaning to ring you.

JANE Leave it out, Viv. That's what I say to my Aunt Matilda.

VIV No, really. We were talking about you only the other day.

JANE What?

VIV How you are. If you're still going round with what's-hisface.

JANE No. I'm footloose and fancy free – so, if it's a night out you're after . . .

VIV My trappin' days are over.

JANE Mine aren't – spoilsport. It's really boring now. There's no-one else mind reads like you and me did – our signals.

VIV At twenty metres in a crowded disco.

JANE See if we can still do it.

Dumbshow: how they could dance and give each other the nod and wink about whether to get off, or get out.
They can still do it.

JANE Go on, then. Get your coat.

VIV *laughs. Those days are over.*

VIV Anyway, Garry'll be home soon.

JANE Suit yourself. I can't tonight, anyway. I've got something on.

VIV How about going for a drink and a pizza? One night next week?

JANE Which night?

VIV I'll see what Garry's got on and I'll give you a ring.

There is an awkward pause, then VIV *and* JANE *speak at the same time.*

VIV He's been working . . .

JANE Is it because I . . .

JANE Go on.

VIV No, you.

JANE Does he not want me coming round?

VIV No! *(I.e. 'That's not it'.)*

JANE I just thought I might as well say it. Clear the air.

VIV I know you don't like him.

JANE I never said that.

VIV People's friends never like the person they end up with.

JANE I never said that.

VIV You took the piss out of him, though.

JANE Can't he spare half an ounce of piss? *(Pause.)* All I said was it seemed to me a bit premature at 25 . . .

VIV That wasn't *all* you said.

JANE . . . to be planning a retirement at 45.

VIV You're always planning.

JANE Not a quarter of a century in advance. Not down to which hacienda in Italy I'll retire to.

VIV *(Pause.)* He's bought me this linguaphone set.

JANE Is that what you get up to – sitting in bed, 'Buenos Noches, darlin', how are your adjectival endings?'

VIV We thought if one of us learns Italian really well, we'll have a head start.

The phone rings, and rings.

JANE I should think you will. Even I'd be able to order a few pizzas if I spent twenty years practising. What will one more language take you, twenty days?

They listen to the phone. VIV *answers* JANE's *unspoken question.*

VIV Obscene caller. Garry doesn't like me to be upset.

JANE *raises her eyebrows, then herself, and strides across to the phone round the other side of the arch in the kitchen.*

JANE *(Picks up phone.)* 'ello?

VIV Don't!

JANE You are calling about ze Italian lessons?

VIV Anyway, that's French.

JANE Oh, sorry, Mrs Benson. No, it's Jane, I'll pass you over. *(To* VIV*.)* Viv, it's your mum – Dumbo!

VIV *takes the phone.* JANE *takes off her cape, reveals her kung-fu outfit and limbers up.*

VIV Hello, Mum? *(Pause.)* No, no , I'm sorry we didn't make it. Garry had some friends round from work. *(Pause.)* No, she just called in. I don't know. *(Pause.)* Yes, yes, I will. And don't forget – ring once, hang up and ring again. All right? 'Bye.

VIV *turns round and sees* JANE .

JANE How do I look?

VIV Eat your heart out, Wonder Woman.

JANE Good. *(Does her Wonder Woman tough walk.)*

VIV Are you doing karate?

JANE Karate chopping, judo, Bruce Lee-ing, ju jitsuing, Kumanfuing – I'm doing kung fu. *(Pause.)* Come with me.

VIV Tonight?

JANE Seven o'clock. It's only the second class.

VIV Garry'll be in for his tea soon.

JANE Can't he get his own tea?

VIV He works such long hours.

JANE So do you; so do I.

VIV No, he really does. It's only fair.

JANE I'll show you what you've missed.

VIV He'll be in in a minute.

JANE The first thing you learn is how to fall. Like this. *(*JANE *falls.)* Try it.

VIV My skirt.

JANE Have a go.

VIV *(Having a go.)* I don't know what I reckon to it if the first thing you do is learn how to fall.

JANE *– helping* VIV *with her fall – walks backwards into* GARRY *and knocks the box he is carrying.*

JANE Hello, Garry.

GARRY Jane.

JANE Didn't mean to rattle your light bulbs.

GARRY I don't sell light bulbs.

VIV *gets up and she and* GARRY *kiss. Perhaps she kicks her shoes under the sofa.*

VIV Jane's just showing me some kung fu.

GARRY *(Charming smile.)* And I thought she'd popped round with a knitting pattern.

JANE *returns the charming smile.*

VIV What have you brought?

GARRY It's a combination dimmer switch set with automatic timer. Economical, and confuses would-be intruders.

JANE Is that what all that floodlighting's about downstairs? – Flashed on when I got near the door.

VIV It's security lighting.

GARRY It comes on automatically when anyone gets within four metres of the building.

JANE How does it know?

GARRY It responds to body heat.

VIV He had to set it at a certain height, didn't you, Garry? So it wouldn't light up for cats.

JANE So a cold-blooded cat burglar could pass undetected. I'll remember that. Anyway, I'd better go.

GARRY Don't let me chase you out.

JANE I never let anyone chase me, unless I want to catch them.

VIV Stay for tea.

JANE Need an empty stomach. See you.

VIV *goes to the door with* JANE.

GARRY 'Bye.

VIV Have a good time at your class.

JANE I intend to.

VIV 'Bye, then.

JANE 'Bye.

GARRY *is laughing to himself.*

VIV What's so funny?

GARRY Her, doing kung fu.

VIV I don't see it.

GARRY Self-defence. Who'd attack her?

VIV Garry!

GARRY She's so aggressive.

VIV She's not.

GARRY She does a good imitation.

VIV I might go with her, next week.

GARRY You!

VIV Why not?

GARRY Women who go in for self-defence are simply deluding themselves.

VIV How do you mean?

GARRY Men are always bigger and stronger.

VIV Not always.

GARRY Nine times out of ten. *(Pause.)* What's gonna happen? She'll think she knows how to throw someone. She'll walk down a dark alley on a dark night, and the attacker won't know he's supposed to stand still while she practises the noble art of chucking him over her shoulder.

VIV You don't think it's a good idea, then?

GARRY All right, maybe I'm being a bit flippant. She's a social worker, she probably needs to protect herself from the riff-raff. But you don't need it, Viv. Unless your boss is up to something you haven't told me about.

VIV *gives him a look.*

GARRY Only joking. I like you just the way you are. I don't want you strutting around like some prize fighter.

VIV Well, maybe not.

GARRY You don't need kung fu. You've got me. I'll look after you.

VIV Not twenty-four hours a day.

GARRY A hundred and twenty-four hours a day. I do love you.

VIV Garry, of us two, who said, 'I love you', first? It was me, wasn't it?

GARRY No.

VIV Are you sure?

GARRY No, it would have put me off you. You're not that kind of girl. You wouldn't have said it first.

VIV I'm sure I did, though – at the baths.

GARRY No, I did. On the picnic.

VIV I thought it first, then.

GARRY What's brought all this on?

VIV Just something I read in *Cosmo.*

GARRY *Cosmo!* Come on, Viv.

VIV It said, 'In love, the one who declares first is lost'.

GARRY 'Lost'? What's 'lost'?

VIV Just lost – you know, lost.

GARRY And you think you're lost?

VIV It just made me feel funny.

GARRY I loved you before you even saw me.

VIV How could you?

GARRY First time I came to your company. I was taken along a corridor. It was a warm day and the doors into the offices were open. That's how I saw you, taking dictation, sitting on a straight-backed chair, your legs crossed, perfectly still except for your hand moving across the page. Your head was bowed and your face turned towards me, your mouth ever so slightly open. I loved you.

VIV You didn't even know me.

GARRY I loved you. I love you.

VIV Shall I tell you what it was for me?

He is already manoeuvering her towards the bedroom.

GARRY *(His mouth on hers.)* Tell me.

She tries to change direction, towards the sofa, and frees her mouth long enough to say:

VIV Do you not fancy messin' up the scatter cushions?

GARRY I fancy messin' you . . . in bed.

They go.

Scene Two

Corner of Laurie/Jane's living room – New Year's Eve, Year 1.

Bopping music. JANE, LAURIE *and* VIV *dance together.* GARRY *drinks low alcohol lager, and watches.* VIV *waves to him to come and dance, but he doesn't.* JANE *goes over to persuade* GARRY *to dance.*

LAURIE I was really nervous about meeting you.

VIV Why?

LAURIE The way she talks about you. If you give me the thumbs down, forget it!

VIV Rubbish.

LAURIE Want to bet?

VIV I won't give you the thumbs down.

LAURIE Thanks.

LAURIE *and* VIV *keep dancing.* JANE *gets* GARRY *up.*

VIV Is it true you're an accountant?

LAURIE Is that bad?

VIV Only if you can't add up.

LAURIE I'm a human calculator.

VIV It doesn't seem to fit.

LAURIE What?

VIV Being an accountant and a kung fu instructor.

LAURIE It fits.

At the end of the record, GARRY *smilingly dips out, taking* VIV *with him.* LAURIE *and* JANE *keep on dancing.*

Scene Three

Flat – twenty minutes later.

A door slams as GARRY *and* VIV *come into the flat. There's an atmosphere. She takes off her coat and dumps it on the sofa. He picks it up and straightens it/hangs it up. She reacts. he comes back.*

VIV Why did you have to spoil our first New Year's Eve?

GARRY Me spoil?

VIV Yes – you spoil. I was enjoying myself.

GARRY Obviously.

VIV What's that supposed to mean?

GARRY As if you didn't know.

VIV What am I supposed to have done?

GARRY As if you didn't know.

VIV I'm not a mind reader.

GARRY No. You're a crotch reader.

VIV What?

GARRY 'What, what, what.' Don't act the innocent.

VIV That low alcohol lager's addled your brain.

GARRY He was itching after you, and you loved it.

VIV Who?

GARRY You were throwing youself at him.

VIV *Who?*

GARRY Laurie.

VIV Laurie!

She starts to laugh.

GARRY I'm glad you find it funny.

VIV I'd no idea you were so jealous.

GARRY Throwing yourself at him, flaunting yourself.

VIV 'Flaunting'? What's this 'flaunting'?

GARRY All right, I'll give it to you in words of one syllable – whore. You were acting like a whore.

VIV Oh, was I now? Really? Is that what you think? Well, all I can say is you've never seen me in action. Try this, tightarse. *(She comes towards him provocatively. He turns away.)* Hello, Laurie. Fancy showing me how to fall, Mr Kumanfu Instructor?

GARRY Don't push it.

VIV Fancy getting into a no-holds-barred combat situation?

GARRY Don't.

VIV Stand still and I'll throw you onto my scatter cushions, big boy.

He hits her and sends her spinning across the room. She ends up sitting on the floor by the sofa. It's very quiet. He doesn't look at her. She doesn't look at him.

VIV You're crazy. I've never looked at anyone else since I met you.

The silence holds. Then he looks at her, sitting there.

GARRY Get up.

VIV Never, never, never.

GARRY Get up.

VIV You knocked me down, you pick me up.

GARRY You're drunk.

VIV You knocked me down, you pick me up! And I never, never, never.

GARRY Don't be stupid.

VIV You've hurt me.

GARRY Let me see.

VIV Hurt me. Laurie? You're nuts.

GARRY I thought . . .

VIV Thought. Thought. Thought followed a hearse and thought it was a wedding.

GARRY Oh, Viv. Come on.

VIV No.

GARRY Oh, Viv. Viv!

VIV There was no need to say those things.

GARRY All right, I'm sorry. *(Pause.)* Come on. Don't make me grovel. *(He helps her up.)* Why did we have to go to their party? *(Pause.)* I didn't want to go. You know that.

VIV There was no need to hit me.

GARRY I'm sorry. *(Pause.)* It's always the same whenever she has anything to do with it.

VIV Who?

GARRY You know.

VIV Jane?

GARRY We end up rowing. She doesn't like me and I don't like her.

VIV So how do you think I feel?

GARRY Well, then why put us through it?

VIV She's my friend.

GARRY I'm your friend, aren't I?

VIV Yes.

GARRY It's you and me now, right?

VIV Yes.

GARRY Stop seeing her.

VIV Stop seeing her.

GARRY She's the past, we're the future.

VIV Stop seeing her altogether?

GARRY You don't have to make a big deal of it. When she rings, I'll say you're not in. I'll say you'll ring back. I can't bear us to fall out like this. *(Pause.)* It's not worth it is it?

VIV No.

GARRY I couldn't bear to see you dancing with him. I wouldn't have hit you if I didn't love you so much. Do you believe me?

VIV I think so.

GARRY Think so? You know so. I panic at the thought that something will go wrong for us.

VIV Nothing is going to go wrong.

GARRY She'll come between us. Stop seeing her, Viv.

VIV All right.

GARRY I love you.

VIV I know.

GARRY And you'll stop seeing her – yes?

VIV I've said so.

GARRY Say it as if you mean it.

VIV If it's that important to you, I'll stop seeing her.

Scene Four

Corner of Laurie/Jane's living room – midnight, New Year's Eve.

Big Ben strikes on the radio or television.

JANE Happy New Year!

LAURIE Happy New Year!

JANE Where's Viv?

Scene Five

Flat – an evening in July, Year 2. Also, corner of kung fu practice hall.

Sofa slantways across room. Hoover abandoned. A tower of old newspapers and magazines has collapsed. VIV *emerges, six and a half months pregnant and carrying baby clothes. She takes out a couple of garments to see how they look. She goes back into the bedroom.*

Meanwhile, JANE *jogs into a corner of the kung fu practice hall, carrying a mat which she places on the floor. She is ready to start.*

JANE Laurie? Laurie?

JANE *goes.*

GARRY *comes in, carrying his briefcase, and looks at the mess.*

GARRY Viv!

VIV *(From bedroom.)* In here!

GARRY Viv!

VIV *(Emerges.)* I didn't expect you home yet.

GARRY So I see. What happened to the light in the hall?

VIV The bulb went.

He goes into the bedroom. She follows him halfway across the room, about to speak. Stops. Waits. Turns back and winds cord round Hoover. He comes back, carrying a light bulb.

VIV I tried to change it.

GARRY I've told you not to change bulbs.

VIV I thought it was a screw type; it was a prong . . .

GARRY *stops, waits.*

VIV I broke the fitting.

He goes and looks for himself. She follows.

VIV When I realised it was a prong, I tried to get it out.

GARRY You have – you've broken it. Why don't you just leave well alone?

VIV Do you not think it'll mend?

GARRY No.

VIV I'll get another one.

GARRY It was a one-off – a sample. I told you.

VIV Something like it.

GARRY You couldn't afford anything remotely resembling this fitting. I'm not putting up with this. I'm not coming home to this.

VIV It was an accident.

GARRY *(Of the living room.)* What's this, an accident? What's the bedroom, an accident?

VIV I'm in the middle . . .

GARRY Of what? The place is a tip.

VIV I was feeling a bit better this afternoon. It was too late to go to work. I started to hoover, in the hall. When the bulb went, and I couldn't change it, I came in here to hoover, but I spilt my tea . . .

GARRY *sees the wet carpet.*

. . . and I didn't want to electrocute myself with the Hoover on the damp carpet, so I thought I'd have a sort out. There was nowhere to put anything, so I thought I'd just do our bedroom.

GARRY Have you touched my papers?

VIV No. *(Pause.)* We've got so much stuff. So then I thought, if I could clear a space in the spare room – just until we decorate.

GARRY The spare room, as well.

VIV We've accumulated so much stuff in such a short time.

GARRY Of course it looks as if we've accumulated a lot, if you spread it across every floor in the flat.

VIV *sits down.*

GARRY Don't sit down. Clear up this mess.

VIV I feel sick.

GARRY So do I, and I've been working all day. I haven't paid for this carpet, and you pour tea all over it.

VIV I sponged it with cold water. It shouldn't stain.

GARRY It better not.

VIV *(Pause.)* I don't know where to start. Everything's getting on top of me.

GARRY Start by drying the carpet.

VIV How, when it's tacked down?

GARRY You've tried to rip the carpet up?

VIV It'll dry itself.

GARRY Dry it before the underfelt rots. Use the hair dryer. *(He passes her the hairdryer.)* Do me a favour. If you're not willing to do housework, say so. I'll do it myself at the weekend. The whole flat would only take an hour.

The hairdryer won't reach the damp patch. GARRY *just looks at* VIV *as if she's sub-normal and he's the master race.* GARRY *spots a broken cup behind the scatter cushions as he moves the sofa.*

GARRY What's this?

VIV The cup fell off the handle.

GARRY So you hid it behind the cushions?

VIV I scalded my arm.

GARRY It's been glued.

VIV It broke before and I glued it. I forgot I'd glued it and it broke. That's when I scalded my arm.

GARRY Why did you hide it?

VIV I didn't want to look at it. *(Pause.)* I liked those cups. I tried to get replacements, but it's a discontinued line.

GARRY How many have you broken?

VIV A few.

GARRY How many?

VIV There's a weakness in the handle. That's probably why they're discontinued, but I liked them.

GARRY How many did we have?

VIV Six.

GARRY How many have you broken?

VIV Six.

GARRY Put it in the bin.

VIV No!

GARRY Put it in the bin.

VIV I thought I'd keep them.

GARRY Put it in the bin.

VIV I thought I'd grow something in them, on the windowsill.

GARRY I'm not having rows of broken cups on the windowsill. Put it in the bin.

VIV Parsley. I thought I'd grow parsley.

He grabs her arm, twists it up her back and forces her towards the bin in the kitchen. She cries out in pain as, meanwhile . . .

Scene Six

Corner of kung fu practice hall – the same evening.

JANE *throws* LAURIE.

JANE Aaa-eee-iii!

LAURIE No yelling, I told you.

JANE It helps.

LAURIE You'll forget and do it in class.

JANE Okay.

LAURIE The aim is to develop skills, and perfect technique – that's all.

JANE Right.

LAURIE It's not about aggression.

JANE So you said.

LAURIE Your aim is to overcome your opponent without incurring injury. Think of it as a physical game of chess.

JANE I'm not interested in chess.

She throws him again – they go.

SCENE SEVEN

Flat – later that evening.

VIV *wears dark glasses. She has just let her mum in.* MUM *watches as* VIV *zips up her overnight bag.*

VIV Mum, I rang to see if you were in, so I could come round – not for you to come here.

MUM What's the matter? Vivienne, what's he done to you?

VIV I thought I'd come and stay, that's all.

MUM What's going on?

VIV He's away . . . overnight. I don't want to be on my own.

MUM Why are you wearing dark glasses indoors?

VIV I bumped into the garage door.

MUM You haven't got a garage.

VIV You don't have to own a garage to bump into a garage door.

MUM No, but it helps.

VIV Let's go.

MUM Sit down, love. Tell me what's wrong.

VIV I'll tell you at home.

MUM Let me look. *(She tries to inspect* VIVS' *bruised cheek and darkening eye.* VIV *draws back, winces.)* Your poor cheek! That eye! Have you got witch hazel?

VIV No. Look all you like when we get home.

MUM All right, but it's not so easy to talk there. I've got a houseful. *(Pause.)* Brian's son has come to stay.

VIV In my room?

MUM Well, yes, because – you know – Ann's got the spare room. *(Pause.)* But of course you can come home, if you need to. *(Pause.)* He's hit you.

VIV Yes.

MUM What for?

VIV What for, what for?

MUM Why did he hit you?

VIV Ask him.

MUM I'm asking you.

VIV I just want to come home.

MUM Leave him?

VIV Yes. No. I don't know.

MUM Of course you can come home. I just don't want you to do anything hasty, that's all.

VIV I want a night in my own bed. *(Pause.)* I don't mind sleeping on the sofa – as long as you don't tell them. I couldn't bear them looking at me, feeling sorry for me.

MUM I can make up the sofa in five minutes.

VIV You've let them take over the house.

MUM I thought you were settled. Are you sure it's not just a hiccup? It happens when women are pregnant. Men have to make adjustments. I'm sure you've got a good' un there.

VIV He'd no right to hit me.

MUM Of course not. But don't over-react, don't throw everything away. You're entitled to be here. *(Pause.)* You've probably given in to him too much.

VIV Sure you're not talking about you and Brian?

MUM You can't give in to them too much or you make a rod for your own back. You're entitled to be here. It's your flat as well.

VIV I don't want to argue. I just want to go.

MUM What was it about? What happened?

GARRY *(From the doorway.)* Tell her, Viv. *(Pause.)* We fell out about the state of the flat. She breaks everything. Messes the place up. But it doesn't matter – it was stupid. It was unimportant. *(He produces flowers from behind his back.)* I'm sorry.

This is a great relief to MUM.

VIV Where do you get flowers at this time of night?

MUM I better leave you two to make up.

VIV Mum!

MUM He's trying to make up.

VIV You don't understand. He hurt me as much as he could. He punched me. He twisted my arm up my back so I couldn't move. He twisted it until I thought my arm would come out of its socket. I blacked out, Mum.

GARRY I didn't mean to hurt you. I didn't realise. I *wouldn't* hurt you.

VIV He did. *(Pause.)* I don't want to lose my baby.

GARRY Our baby. Oh, Viv, I'm so sorry. I couldn't bear to lose you. I'm such a fool. It wasn't meant. None of it was meant. Don't go. You won't have to lift a finger between now and the time the baby's born, I swear on my mother's life. Talk to her, Mrs Benson, please.

MUM You'll have to learn to keep your temper.

GARRY I know.

MUM You shouldn't expect too much of Vivienne. Not so soon. Not when she's pregnant.

GARRY I know. I'll never forgive myself.

MUM You both have to work at a marriage. Vivienne, you have to try to keep the place nice – a nice home.

VIV You're the perfect housekeeper, not me.

MUM I should have let you do more for yourself. I was always picking up after you. *(Pause.)* All you have to do is put things away as you use them – have a routine.

VIV I try.

MUM I should have come round, helped you with the housework.

GARRY There's no need for that, is there, Viv?

VIV Mum, it's not your fault.

GARRY Put yourself in my shoes – I could have stayed in Carlisle. I drove all the way back like a maniac and into this.

MUM Let me clear up.

GARRY No, no. I'll do it.

VIV I'm so useless.

GARRY Things'll be better. I know they will. Say you'll forgive me, Viv. It won't happen again.

VIV Promise?

GARRY I promise.

MUM There. I was so worried. I was sick with worry on the way over. And Brian doesn't know where I am. *(To* VIV.*)* I won't say anything to anyone. But he'll think I've got lost.

GARRY How're you getting home?

MUM I'll get the bus.

GARRY You will not. You're not walking the streets at this time of night, I'll take you. *(To* VIV.*)* Do you want to come for the ride.

VIV No.

GARRY I'll be back soon.

MUM *(Kisses* VIV.*)* I know how it feels like the end of the world, but it's not.

GARRY *(Kisses* VIV.*)* I don't expect you to be perfect. I just want you to try.

VIV *watches* GARRY *and* MUM *go, then takes her overnight bag back into the bedroom.*

SCENE EIGHT

Flat – a hot morning in June, Year 3.

DOCTOR *and* VIV *come from the bedroom.*

VIV I'm sorry if I've called you out for no reason, Doctor.

DOCTOR I know the first baby's a worry, and I don't mind coming out.

VIV Why should she get a chill in summer? Am I doing something wrong, or what?

DOCTOR No, you're not doing anything wrong. It's common enough. Just keep Sarah warm . . .

VIV Sara. Sara Jane.

DOCTOR . . . and give her plenty of liquids.

VIV Liquids, all right, and keep her warm. Garry'll be relieved. He sings her to sleep.

DOCTOR *smiles.*

VIV I wish someone would sing me to sleep. I'm so tired all the time.

DOCTOR Try to sleep when she sleeps.

VIV But I'm in such a state. I worry. Like I'm waiting for something to go wrong.

DOCTOR Do you want something to relax you?

VIV I don't like taking things – pills, tablets.

DOCTOR But if you're not resting.

VIV It was better before. I arranged to go part time after she was born and it was fine. I was tired, but I was managing. I had my job. Then, couple of times, I had to miss. I was so tired, my head was so bad. I was aching all over, all down my back. I must have lifted something the wrong way.

DOCTOR Is your back still bothering you?

VIV Sometimes.

DOCTOR If you come down to the surgery, I'll examine you. I have another call to make just now.

VIV Oh, I'm sorry. I'm wittering.

DOCTOR No.

VIV No, all I was saying . . . I lost my job, you see. I rang in sick and, of course, my husband, Garry, he forgot I was home and he called in to see me at work. Made me look a liar. And my boss, we were so busy with the Cologne contract, and he couldn't – I lost my job.

DOCTOR I shouldn't worry about it. You've got enough on your hands now, eh?

VIV I'm not coping very well. Then there's my leg.

DOCTOR Your leg?

VIV It won't stop bleeding.

DOCTOR Let me see. *(Pause.)* How did this happen?

VIV *(Pause.)* I walked into the garage door.

DOCTOR The garage door?

VIV Yes.

DOCTOR And you've a bruise. *(Pause.)* If you come down to the surgery at two, Dr Craven will put a couple of stitches in your leg.

VIV All right.

DOCTOR Is there anything else?

VIV Just, just my nerves.

DOCTOR I see.

VIV Maybe I'd better take the prescription, for my nerves.

DOCTOR I'll leave a prescription at reception for you. Unless you change your mind.

(Pause.)

VIV No, I mean I need something – a prescription.

DOCTOR Right. I'll see myself out then.

VIV *watches her go, and then goes back to Sara Jane.*

VIV It's all right. Mummy's coming.

SCENE NINE

Flat – Christmas Eve, Year 3.

Tree and poshly wrapped presents. GARRY *at his paperwork.*

GARRY Where've you been?

VIV Where's Tracey, didn't she tell you?

GARRY You know I don't like Tracey baby sitting.

VIV But she was here?

GARRY She said you'd taken her mum to see her dad in hospital.

VIV Yes.

GARRY Why couldn't she take herself?

VIV She doesn't drive. I drove her, in their car.

GARRY Hospital visiting ends at eight o'clock.

VIV She was in a state, she wanted to talk. She wanted to go for a drink.

GARRY You've been drinking?

VIV I had a bitter lemon. She just needed to talk.

GARRY What about?

VIV About him, about the situation . . .

GARRY And what about you?

VIV Me? What about me?

GARRY What did you talk about?

VIV Nothing.

GARRY Nothing?

VIV She did all the talking.

GARRY What did she say?

VIV About him? This, that, you know, what the doctor said, what she said, how bad he is.

GARRY So you never said a word.

VIV No. All I kept saying was, 'I know, I know'.

GARRY What have you been telling her?

VIV Nothing.

GARRY You've been talking about us.

VIV No! Oh, she's heard you, if that's what you're getting at. She envies us our 'tempestuous relationship'.

GARRY If you talk to her about us . . .

VIV I don't.

GARRY If I find out you've been talking, I'll drop you from that window.

VIV I'm too ashamed to talk.

She goes. He follows her out of the room.

SCENE TEN

Cafe – table by the window – an afternoon in April, Year 5.

JANE Laurie, we have to ring back this afternoon and say yea or nay.

LAURIE I don't know.

JANE You don't know. So, I go on getting ground down at work, and you go on totting up figures . . .

LAURIE We're secure.

JANE . . . renting the church hall . . .

LAURIE It's not a church hall.

JANE . . . or we take a chance.

LAURIE A leap in the dark.

JANE We're talking about managing a sports centre, not jumping off a cliff.

LAURIE I'm not sure.

JANE We can make a go of it – together.

LAURIE If it was just somewhere where we knew people.

JANE You're scared.

LAURIE All right, I'm scared.

JANE Be brave.

LAURIE I don't feel brave.

JANE I don't want to have to drag you kicking and screaming out of your rut . . . Are you listening?

LAURIE Look! Friend of yours there.

LAURIE *dashes out of the cafe and catches up with* VIV *who's laden down with shopping.*

LAURIE Viv!

VIV Laurie! What a surprise.

LAURIE Come and have a cup of tea with us.

VIV I'm on my way to pick Sara Jane up from nursery.

LAURIE *(Steering* VIV *into the cafe.)* Come on, five minutes – you look as if you could use it.

JANE Hello, stranger.

VIV *(Sitting down.)* Hello, Jane. You look well. You both look well.

LAURIE I'll get you a cup of tea.

JANE How are you?

VIV Oh, you know. Fine. Just been shopping.

JANE So I see.

VIV I'm making something a bit special for our wedding anniversary.

JANE Oh, right. It's that time of year.

VIV Five years. I bought some trout.

JANE Good.

VIV I was just looking in that kitchen shop next door. Have you seen it.

JANE I haven't been in.

VIV You name it, they've got it. Metal steamers, bamboo steamers, poachers for three eggs, enamel collanders, vegetable strainers, potato peelers – and so many knives. Peeling knives, scraping knives, carving knives, chopping knives – and this, I bought this. *(Shows a short sharp glinting knife.)*

JANE That looks useful.

VIV That's what I thought. I thought you could keep it in your apron pocket in the kitchen.

JANE If he gives you any bother, you mean. *(Pause.)* Only joking.

LAURIE *gives* VIV *tea.*

VIV Thanks. I can only stay a minute, I'm on my way to pick Sara Jane up.

JANE How is she?

VIV She's fine. She gets on very well, and she's no trouble.

JANE How's Garry?

VIV He's fine. He was promoted to Area Manager.

JANE So Italy gets nearer.

VIV Not really.

JANE You must be brilliant at Italian by now.

VIV I don't seem to be able to concentrate these days.

JANE But you have a flair for languages.

VIV Only French and German.

LAURIE Only, she says. You're a bilingual secretary, aren't you?

VIV I haven't worked for a while. *(Pause.)* Do you know what I'm always remembering? When we worked in France.

LAURIE She doesn't tell me about that.

VIV We got into so many tight corners – but we had this motto: never apologise; never explain.

JANE And we never did. *(Laughs.)* Our little catch phrases.

VIV Take what life has to offer.

JANE Refuse nothing but blows.

LAURIE Come on, then – dish the dirt.

JANE Viv used to rescue me all the time.

VIV Did I?

JANE You had to – I couldn't speak French. When I tried, I used to make it worse.

VIV Still, I wouldn't have dared go if it hadn't been for you.

JANE I don't know why.

VIV Not on my own. You were always the one for doing things.

JANE Such as?

VIV Going to kung fu classes. *(Pauses.)* Do you remember that night you asked me to go and I said no?

JANE Did you? I didn't think you gave me an answer.

LAURIE I was the attraction there.

JANE Don't flatter yourself. I didn't know who it was going to be.

LAURIE You just got lucky.

JANE I almost didn't come that second week – all those blokes. You.

LAURIE I thought I was very good.

JANE That's not the point. I don't know – you two, between you. You just see me as . . . If you really want to know, I went to kung fu because I was shit scared. I nearly got done in. It was a Friday night in August, I'd been to the disco, got off the late bus on the corner of our road and the avenue, and this bloke got off behind me and started to walk in the same direction, keeping pace, a few steps behind. I walked faster, he walked faster. I started to run, he started to run. I forgot to breathe. I knew if he caught me, I wouldn't have the breathe to scream. I wouldn't be able to move. It was like I was frozen inside. My heart had stopped and it was lying in the pit of my gut, and my heels tapping out: here she is, here she is. As I got nearer home, I tried to get my keys but my hands were shaking and I dropped them and lost time picking them up. I tried to scream, but nothing came out. I got my key in the lock, and then I felt his hands on my throat. Somehow I managed to turn the key, and the dog barked, and he ran off. I slammed the door shut and I just collapsed on the floor, shaking. That was why I decided to go to kung fu.

LAURIE *(Pause.)* I didn't know that.

JANE Yeah, well.

VIV *(Getting up quickly.)* Sorry, I have to go. I have to pick Sara Jane up – I'm late – I didn't realise the time – I'm so late.

LAURIE 'Bye Viv. *(*VIV *exits. Pause.)* Don't let her get to you.

JANE She couldn't. I don't know her any more.

Scene Eleven

Flat – a week later – morning.

VIV *is dressed, and comes out of the kitchen as* GARRY *comes from the bedroom, fastening his tie – ready for work.*

GARRY You're up early.

VIV Morning, Dr Jekyll.

GARRY What?

VIV Dr Jekyll, Mr Hyde.

GARRY Coffee?

VIV I'm not supposed to say, am I? If you decide to be nice, I'm supposed to thank my lucky stars.

GARRY Give it a rest.

VIV You upset Sara Jane last night.

GARRY Rubbish!

VIV You know you did. She tried to stop you, you wouldn't stop.

GARRY Leave it.

VIV That look on her face.

GARRY Let it drop.

VIV She knew.

GARRY Don't I get any breakfast today?

VIV She knew. Don't you see . . .?

GARRY Where were you this morning? I reached out for you.

She backs away.

I wanted you, you weren't there. I never get any love any more.

VIV Don't!

GARRY Come on, time for a quickie. Take your mind off things.

VIV Don't.

GARRY Come on, sweetheart.

VIV Sara . . .

GARRY So? You don't want her getting upset again.

VIV Don't touch me.

GARRY Come on, easy does it. *(He gets* VIV *in a clinch and feels the knife in her pocket.)* What's this?

She gets it first and holds it, threatening.

VIV Get out!

GARRY What's got into you?

VIV I can't take it any more.

GARRY Calm down.

VIV If you touch me, I'll kill you!

GARRY What are you – mental?

VIV I've nothing to lose any more.

He picks briefcase/something up, and they circle the room.

GARRY You are – you're mental!

VIV Don't come any nearer!

GARRY You say I upset Sara, so you pull a knife on me while she's in the next room.

VIV She was in the same room last night – you could have killed me.

GARRY Put it down.

VIV Get out! Get out of here!

He lunges, hits the knife out of her hand. There's a struggle. He gets the knife and holds it to her throat.

VIV Oh, so it's me . . . It's gonna be me . . . It'd have to be me . . . Go on then, kill me!

GARRY Now why would I want to do that? *(Putting knife in his pocket.)* I'll take Sara to nursery this morning.

VIV She hasn't had her breakfast.

GARRY I'll take her to the Little Chef on the way in.

VIV No.

GARRY What's wrong with the Little Chef?

VIV I take her to nursery.

GARRY You're not fit to look after a child.

VIV I take her.

GARRY Look at you. Look at your crazy eyes. You want to go out and play the wounded soldier. You're staying here. *(Going.)* Come on, sweetheart. Daddy's taking you to nursery today.

VIV *just stands where she is. He goes out. The outside door shuts.*

After a few seconds, VIV *goes to the door, tries to open it. The door is locked. She bangs on it and yells after him.*

VIV Wait! Sara! Garry, the deadlock! You've locked me in. *(Pause.)* You bastard! *(Pause.)*

She goes into the kitchen and picks up the phone. Dials 999.

Police. Put me through to the police.

Scene Twelve

Flat – an hour later.

JANE *and* LAURIE *come into the flat.*

LAURIE So, where is she?

JANE Viv? Laurie, what's happened?

LAURIE Viv!

VIV *comes out of the bedroom.*

JANE Viv?

VIV I didn't know if you'd come.

JANE What's going on?

VIV I didn't know who else to ring. I didn't even know if you'd be at home – I didn't know your number at work.

JANE What is it?

VIV I need a lift.

JANE Where to?

VIV To pick Sara Jane up . . . And somewhere to stay, just for a few days.

LAURIE But we're moving, we're packing up.

JANE *stops him.*

JANE Of course you can stay.

LAURIE *gives her a look – where?*

LAURIE What happened to the doors? Did someone break in?

VIV The police. I was locked in, and I called them. I was going to tell them, but when it came to it, I couldn't. I couldn't say anything. This morning, I wanted to kill him, but when it came to it . . . I knew I had to go, and take . . . I was going to tell them, but . . . Bad as he is, I . . . I kept thinking, what if he loses his job, loses me, loses Sara . . .

JANE What were you going to tell the police?

VIV Can't you guess?

JANE Can't you say?

LAURIE Say what?

Pause.

VIV He beats me up.

LAURIE What?

VIV He beats me up.

JANE Come on. Let's go.

GARRY *in the doorway.*

GARRY Where do you think you're going?

VIV What are you . . .? How did you . . .?

GARRY The police rang me at work. Said you seemed upset. What's the matter? Couldn't you find your key. What? What is it? You're always losing your key. Come on, I'll make you a cup of tea and call a locksmith. Thanks for coming round, you two, but everything's under control now.

VIV I'm leaving.

GARRY What do you mean, leaving?

VIV Leaving you.

GARRY That's a bit rash.

JANE Come on, Viv.

GARRY Don't be silly. You wouldn't survive without me. Viv, you need me.

JANE Viv.

GARRY If you go, you don't come back.

VIV I won't. (*Pause.*) My bag.

JANE Laurie, give us a minute.

VIV *and* JANE *go into the bedroom.* LAURIE *sits down on the sofa.*

GARRY This is my flat. (*Pause.*) Get out, or I'll call the police.

LAURIE I'll go when Viv says so.

GARRY This is ridiculous.

LAURIE Yeah.

GARRY You don't know what she's like.

LAURIE I don't care, you've no right to hit her. That doesn't give you a right to hit her.

GARRY You don't come between a man and his wife, you know that. This isn't your fight.

LAURIE It's not on. It's got to finish.

GARRY I haven't even started.

VIV *and* JANE *come out of the bedroom with an overnight bag.*

GARRY Ask them – ask them how long they'll put up with you.

VIV I'll sleep on the pavement.

GARRY Is that how much you think of Sara Jane?

VIV It's because of Sara . . . I don't know why I didn't . . .

JANE *takes* VIV'S *arm and they are on their way out.*

GARRY Maybe it's for the best. You're not fit to look after her.

VIV *turns.*

GARRY You're not thinking of taking her with you? No way. How would you feed her? Clothe her? You've no job, you've nowhere to stay, you've no money. You pop pills all day long. Did she tell you that? Do you even know what year we're in?

JANE Come on, Viv.

VIV *hesitates.*

VIV Sara.

Don't Cry Baby

Katie Campbell

Cast

WOMAN

MAN

MOTHER

FRIEND

WOMAN 2

WOMAN 3

Each character has an icon:

woman – bottle
man – hat
mother – apron
friend – bouquet of flowers.

Initially the icon identifies the character: actors switch character by switching icons. Later icons will be used as props, i.e.:

hat = potty, bowl, pregnant stomach
bottle = glass, sample jar, baby
apron = nappy, paper package, towel
bouquet = broom, baby.

Stage is bare except for a crate which is used as a chair, table and bed. Action should be snappy, slap-stick, acrobatic; scene changes have a quick blackout. Rhymes should not be stressed.

Scene One

All four actors walk in a circle round the icons. Before s/he speaks, each actor picks up the icon which represents her/his character and after speaking, s/he returns it to the centre.

MAN The time is right.

WOMAN The time is wrong.

MOTHER The time has come.

WOMAN The time will pass.

MAN The time is now.

WOMAN I need more time.

MAN There is no time.

MOTHER There's no time like . . .

MAN I'm out of time.

WOMAN There will be time.

MOTHER Time's running on.

MAN Time's running out.

MOTHER Time doesn't wait.

WOMAN Time doesn't end.

MAN Time doesn't stop.

MOTHER 'Time's winged . . .'

WOMAN 'Life: time's fool.'

MOTHER Time flies.

Momentary pause. All stop, poised.

WOMAN Time doesn't fly?

MOTHER Doesn't time fly? (*Throws hat to* MAN.)

MAN When you're having fun.

Scene Two

WOMAN I don't want to do it.

MAN Never?

WOMAN Not now.

MAN Ever?

WOMAN Someday. Maybe. Not today.

MAN When?

WOMAN Next week? Next month? Next year?

WOMAN No. I don't know.

MAN I want it now.

WOMAN Too bad for you.

MAN I need you to.

WOMAN I'm sad for you.

They switch.

MAN I need you to do it for me.

WOMAN For you?

MAN For me.

WOMAN For you!

MAN For us.

They switch.

WOMAN I won't.

MAN You will.

WOMAN I won't.

MAN You must.

WOMAN I won't.

MAN You shall.

WOMAN Says who?

MAN You.

WOMAN Me!

MAN It was understood.

WOMAN By whom.

MAN You knew. You always knew. You knew I always wanted to.

WOMAN *(Concedes, change of mood.)* Yes, I'm sorry. I can't do it.

MOTHER *enters.*

MOTHER Do it for me.

MAN Do it for her.

MOTHER Do it for him.

FRIEND *enters.*

FRIEND Do it for you.

FRIEND *switches with woman.*

FRIEND *(Whispers.)* Don't do it.

MAN Do it.

Change of mood. MAN *and* WOMAN *switch.*

FRIEND Do it. Don't tell him; just do it.

MAN Don't you dare. You're not ready.

FRIEND *(To* MAN.*)* Do you care?

WOMAN *You're* not ready.

MAN I'm not ready.

MAN *switches with* MOTHER.

MAN We're not ready.

MOTHER You're not ready.

FRIEND *(To* MAN, *whispers.)* She's not ready.

MOTHER *(To* WOMAN, *whispers.)* He's not ready.

FRIEND *(To* MOTHER, *whispers.)* They're not ready.

MAN *(To* FRIEND, *whispers.)* You're not ready.

FRIEND I'm not ready!

WOMAN *(To* FRIEND.*)* You stay out of this.

MAN This isn't your affair.

WOMAN *and* FRIEND *switch.*

MAN *(To* WOMAN, *angry.)* This isn't her affair.

WOMAN *(To* FRIEND, *apologetic.)* This isn't your affair.

FRIEND *(To* MOTHER.*)* This isn't my affair.

WOMAN *(To* MOTHER, *angry.)* This isn't your affair.

MAN *(To* MOTHER, *angry.)* You stay out of this.

FRIEND *(To* MOTHER, *sympathetic.)* It isn't your affair.

WOMAN *(To* MAN, *angry.)* You stay out of this.

WOMAN *switches with* MAN.

WOMAN It isn't your affair.

MAN It isn't my affair.

MAN *switches with* MOTHER.

MAN It *is* my affair!

MAN *switches with* FRIEND.

MAN Of course it's my affair.

MAN *switches with* WOMAN.

MAN Who else's affair is it?

MAN *switches with* MOTHER.

MAN It's only my affair.

MAN *switches with* WOMAN.

MAN This is between you and me. Not her. Or her. Or her. It's my affair and your affair and that's all there is to it.

SCENE THREE

All retrieve icons from centre except WOMAN'S *bottle, which is grabbed by* MOTHER *before* WOMAN *can get it.*

MOTHER *(Throws bottle at* WOMAN.*)* That's all there is to it.

MAN *(Throws hat at* WOMAN.*)* See, there's nothing to it.

FRIEND *(Throws bouquet at* WOMAN.*)* Nothing to it.

WOMAN *(Struggling to catch and hold all the icons.)* That's all there is to it?

MOTHER *(Removes aprons, sweeps all icons into it, folds it up neatly.)* That's all there is to it.

WOMAN *(Picks up apron parcel, spilling contents – deliberately? angrily?)* That's all there is to it. *(Drops apron over the spilled icons.)*

Scene Four

MAN You owe it to me.

WOMAN I owe it to me.

MOTHER You owe it to me.

FRIEND You owe it to me.

MAN What about your mother . . .

FRIEND . . . Your parents . . .

MAN . . .*My* parents.

WOMAN What about my parents?

WOMAN *switches with* MAN.

MAN Your mother's getting old.

WOMAN Your father's getting old.

MAN We're getting old.

WOMAN You're getting old.

MAN You're getting old.

WOMAN I am not getting old!

MAN You're getting older.

WOMAN We're getting older.

MAN You're getting older.

FRIEND She's getting older.

FRIEND *switches with* MOTHER.

WOMAN What if I die?

MOTHER What if I die?

WOMAN I'm not getting old.

WOMAN *switches with* MOTHER.

WOMAN What if I die?

MOTHER There's nothing to it.

MOTHER *switches with* MAN.

MOTHER What if I die?

MOTHER *switches with* MAN *again.*

WOMAN What if I die?

MOTHER There's nothing to it.

MAN Nobody dies these days.

FRIEND They do.

MOTHER They did in my day.

FRIEND It's safer not do it, anyway.

MAN *switches with* WOMAN *.They become children, fighting.*

WOMAN I want it.

MAN I want it.

WOMAN It's yours.

MAN It's not mine, it's yours.

WOMAN It's ours.

MAN It's mine!

WOMAN It's mine!

MAN It's ours.

WOMAN It's mine!

MAN It's mine!

WOMAN It's mine, and you can't take it!

MAN Be careful! You'll break it!

They switch.

MAN It's mine.

WOMAN 'Possession is nine tenths.'

MAN It's mine and I want to hold it.

WOMAN Tough.

MAN What?

WOMAN Tough shit! I might not even have it in the first place – shit-face!

Scene Five

WOMAN We're getting old.

MAN We still have ages.

WOMAN I want it while I'm young enough.

MAN You have to take these things in stages.

WOMAN What's the next stage?

MAN Waiting.

WOMAN All this hesitating!

MAN We can't afford it, anyway.

WOMAN With the Porsches and videos and holidays . . .

MAN We need some time together first.

WOMAN We've had five years. I feel I'm cursed.

MAN Another five, then I'll be bound.

WOMAN I want it while Mother's still around.

MAN Your mother will outlive us all!

WOMAN You never know. Old and all . . .

MAN *(Serious.)* Darling, I don't want it.

FRIEND *and* MOTHER *enter.* WOMAN *switches with* MOTHER. MAN *switches with* FRIEND.

WOMAN *(To* FRIEND.*)* He won't make the commitment.

MOTHER *(To* WOMAN.*)* He can't make the commitment.

FRIEND *(To* WOMAN.*)* He doesn't want to be committed . . .

MAN . . . tied . . .

MOTHER . . . bound . . .

MAN . . . gagged.

WOMAN *(To* FRIEND.*)* Not to me.

FRIEND Not to it.

MAN Not to anyone or anything.

They all turn once around.

MOTHER It's a question of responsibility.

FRIEND *(To* WOMAN.*)* It's your responsibility.

WOMAN *(To* MAN.*)* It's your responsibility.

MAN It's my responsibility.

WOMAN It's my responsibility. I want it, I'll have it. I'll suffer the consequences.

MOTHER *(To* WOMAN.*)* It's your responsibility.

FRIEND *(To* MAN.*)* It's your responsibility.

WOMAN *(To* MAN.*)* It's our responsibility.

MAN It isn't my responsibility.

MAN *switches with* WOMAN.

MAN It's our responsibility.

MOTHER *(To* WOMAN.*)* He's too irresponsible.

FRIEND *(To* MAN.*)* You're too irresponsible.

WOMAN I will be responsible.

MAN I won't be responsible.

MAN *switches with* MOTHER. WOMAN *switches with* FRIEND.

WOMAN I don't want the responsibility.

MAN I'll take the responsibility.

WOMAN You're too irresponsible.

MAN It's my responsibility.

MOTHER *(To* MAN *and* WOMAN.*)* It's your responsibility.

WOMAN It's got nothing to do with me.

They all turn around once.

FRIEND She can't bear to think of herself as a mother.

WOMAN He can't bear to think of himself as a father.

MOTHER She can't bear to think of herself as a mother.

WOMAN It's all I can do to be a daughter. Hell! I don't want to be a mother as well!

WOMAN *switches with* MOTHER.

MOTHER She can't bear to be someone else's mother.

WOMAN He wants me to be his exclusive mother.

FRIEND He can't bear to think of you as somebody's mother.

MOTHER I can't bear to think of you as a mother.

WOMAN I can't bear. I won't bear. I *won't* be a mother.

MOTHER *and* WOMAN *switch.*

MOTHER He wants a mother.

WOMAN He needs a mother.

WOMAN *switches with* MAN.

WOMAN I don't want to be a mother.

MAN You don't want to be a mother.

FRIEND You want her to be a mother.

MOTHER What's wrong with being a mother!

Scene Six

WOMAN I just need . . .

FRIEND I just want . . .

MAN I just . . . I just feel . . .

MAN Just let me get on . . .

WOMAN . . . just a little bit further . . .

FRIEND . . . my next big promotion . . .

MAN . . . one more major deal . . .

WOMAN . . . one contract . . .

MAN . . . two clients . . .

FRIEND . . . three more commissions . . .

MAN . . . just a few more years . . .

FRIEND . . . of promotions . . .

WOMAN . . . security . . .

MAN . . . a promise of tenure to relieve my fears.

Mood change.

MOTHER It will be too late then.

MAN What if you can't?

FRIEND That's what you always say.

WOMAN What if you're impotent?

MOTHER If you're infertile?

MAN What if you're barren?

FRIEND It can take years.

MAN You could be too old, then.

MOTHER You'd be left with nothing.

FRIEND Nothing.

MAN A lonely old age.

FRIEND No-one to care for.

MAN No-one to care for you.

MOTHER No-one to care . . .

FRIEND . . . when you're old and grey . . .

MOTHER . . . when you're dying and dead.

MAN There'd be nobody there.

SCENE SEVEN

MAN It's time.

WOMAN Oh no, please . . .

MOTHER . . . don't start that again.

MAN Do it.

MOTHER Have it.

MAN Take the plunge.

MOTHER A gesture. It's a gesture.

MAN A symbol.

MOTHER An act of faith.

MAN An act of commitment.

MOTHER A re-creation.

MAN A gift for the future.

MOTHER A new generation.

MAN A gesture of permanence.

MOTHER A scoff at mortality.

MAN Ensured immortality.

MOTHER It's future insurance.

WOMAN It's present endurance.

MAN It's what you are here for.

FRIEND It's what you were built for.

WOMAN *(Angry, to* FRIEND.*)* Oh no, not you too!

MOTHER It's what you are destined to do.

Scene Eight

WOMAN *and* FRIEND *alone on stage.*

WOMAN Well, I've done it.

FRIEND What?

WOMAN I've done it.

FRIEND It? (WOMAN *nods.*) No!

WOMAN Yes.

FRIEND Why?

WOMAN I don't know.

FRIEND Why?

WOMAN It was time.

FRIEND Why?

WOMAN It just happened.

FRIEND It doesn't just happen.

WOMAN I didn't intend it . . .

FRIEND You could always prevent it. Do you know what this means?

WOMAN There's never a good enough reason, it seems . . .

FRIEND To have or not?

WOMAN Either. Both. Neither.

The two other actors come on with no icons and switch with WOMAN *and* FRIEND, *who then become* WOMAN 2 *and* WOMAN 3.

FRIEND What about him?

WOMAN He's delighted.

WOMAN 2 *(Steps in.)* He's horrified.

WOMAN 3 He doesn't know.

WOMAN He doesn't care.

WOMAN 2 He doesn't care much one way or the other.

WOMAN 3 It's my decision; he doesn't care.

WOMAN It's my decision.

WOMAN 2 Your burden.

WOMAN 3 Your responsibility.

FRIEND Your mistake.

WOMAN 2 Your body.

WOMAN 3 Your future.

FRIEND Your funeral.

All turn around.

FRIEND What about your career? *(Whispers to someone over her shoulder.)* Finished – that's for sure. *(To* WOMAN.*)* It will present problems, I fear.

WOMAN I'll work something out.

FRIEND *(To audience.)* These women – the presumptions they make! What do they want, for Christ's sake?

MAN You give 'em the chance, the training. They take up the company's money and time, then – just when they begin being productive – it's up and . . . thwack! *(Shakes his head.)*

WOMAN Excuse me. Please, sir. Can I have . . . a minute? A word? There's something I . . . really, I . . .

MAN This is absurd!

WOMAN We must discuss . . . *(*MAN *stops shaking his head,* *turns to listen.)* No problem – the statutory leave, that's all . . . I don't . . . I won't . . . I won't want more. I will be back . . .

MAN *(To audience.)* And will they, hell!

FRIEND In two months.

MOTHER . . . no, four; the first two you're exhausted – can't think any more.

FRIEND In four months, she'll be bored. In six, she'll be depressed. By eight, she'll have lost confidence. By ten, she'll be oppressed. Within a year, she will be . . .

WOMAN No problem. Really, no problem. *(To self.)* I pray . . . *(To* MAN.*)* I'll have it and nurse it and find a child-minder and be back before you know I'm away.

MAN You can't leave a baby . . .

MOTHER . . . a new-born baby . . .

MAN . . . you can't leave a baby . . .

MOTHER . . . all on its own.

FRIEND You've heard of the case in the United States . . .

MAN . . . child molesters.

MOTHER They drug the babies to keep them quiet.

FRIEND They sit them in front of the TV all day.

MOTHER They let them eat candy . . .

FRIEND . . . and beat . . .

MOTHER . . . and abuse . . .

MAN . . . and hit the kids when they cry, they say.

MOTHER You can't leave her now; she's only a baby.

MAN You can't leave him now; he's barely a child.

FRIEND You can't leave them now; they're just about school age.

MOTHER You can't leave them now; they're at the vulnerable stage . . .

MAN . . . the formative period . . .

FRIEND . . . just when they need you.

MOTHER You can't just desert them; just ignore their call.

FRIEND What do you want, girl! You can't have it all.

SCENE NINE

WOMAN *stands alone, dejected, on stage.* FRIEND *enters with flowers.*

FRIEND *(Presents her with the bouquet.)* What's the matter?

WOMAN I'm fine. *(Turns away, arranging flowers in bottle-vase.)*

FRIEND What's the matter?

WOMAN *(Begins retching.)* I'm sick.

MAN *enters.*

MAN It isn't a sickness.

MOTHER *enters.*

MOTHER It's a natural process.

FRIEND It's perfectly healthy. *(Aside.)* You're looking so pale.

WOMAN *grabs* MAN*'s hat and spews into it.*

WOMAN I'm perfectly healthy. I'm just feeling frail.

MOTHER She's fine.

MAN She's all right.

MOTHER She's making a fuss.

MAN A little attention, that's all she needs. *(Bends solicitously towards her.)*

FRIEND *(Aside.)* She's reaping the punishment now for her deeds.

Scene Ten

WOMAN *and* FRIEND *alone on stage.* WOMAN *holds hat to her stomach as the pregnancy bump.*

FRIEND So how does it feel? *(Pointing to the bump.)*

WOMAN It doesn't feel anything.

FRIEND Can I touch? *(Touches gingerly.)* Is there anything there?

WOMAN It feels. Well, it feels. Oh, you know . . . I feel tired.

FRIEND Are you sure you're still sure . . . I mean, you know . . . sometimes . . . There are things we can do; I know where to go . . .

WOMAN It's too late. It's alive now. Everyone knows.

FRIEND Okay. If you say . . .

They turn once around and stand as in opening of scene.

FRIEND So, how does it feel?

WOMAN It doesn't feel anything.

FRIEND Can I feel? It doesn't feel . . . are you sure . . .

WOMAN It feels, it eats – I know, it eats me. It feels, it hears . . .

FRIEND What?

MAN *enters.*

MAN Did you hear?

FRIEND What?

MAN The one about . . .

FRIEND What?

MAN . . . what's blue and sits in a corner?

FRIEND What?

MAN A baby in a plastic bag. What's red and sits in a corner?

FRIEND What?

MAN A baby eating razor blades. What's easier to empty: a lorry load of babies or a lorry load of billiard balls?

FRIEND What?

MAN A lorry load of babies – you can use a pitchfork.

FRIEND Oh my god, that's sick.

MAN Ever seen a nappy full of baby-shit? *That's* sick.

Scene Eleven

WOMAN *–pregnant – and* MOTHER *on stage.*

WOMAN Nobody told me! Why didn't you say!

MOTHER *(Shrugs.)* You do it; you get through it.

WOMAN Why didn't you warn me! You didn't explain!

MOTHER Warning you wouldn't have relieved the pain.

MAN *enters.*

MAN What's this. Old wives tales? Bad for the baby. Don't fill the poor girl full of fear. *(Bends over and kisses her.)* Most natural thing in the world, it is. How else do you think we all got to be here? *(Chuckles. Hands her a bouquet of flowers.)* The workers used to drop them in the fields, then go straight back to work.

MOTHER The gymnasts go through labour without a spasm or jerk.

MAN Nothing to it, it's a breeze. Brave girl like you'll get through with ease.

SCENE TWELVE

Pregnant WOMAN *and* FRIEND *on stage.* WOMAN *squats on hat, with apron rolled in her lap – under her dress – to show the pregnancy.*

WOMAN Constipation.

FRIEND They didn't say.

WOMAN Apricots and bran each day.

FRIEND Prune juice.

WOMAN Uggh! Sometimes, I doubt . . .

FRIEND You're not afraid you're going to . . .

WOMAN What? Miscarry?

FRIEND Shit it out . . .

WOMAN *switches apron bundle with* FRIEND, *tips hat on her head to become* MAN. *From wings, someone throws in the bouquet.*

MAN Now, darling, you mustn't get depressed. There you go . . . It's simply the change in hormones, you know. *(Hands her the bouquet.)* I brought you a present. *(She ignores them.)* Here for you. *(She takes them. He removes his hat. Hands it to her. She puts it over her stomach as baby and uses the bouquet as a broom.)* Now, what's for dinner? *(No reply.)* Anything? Nothing. You didn't go shopping. No. I see. No, it's not that I expect you to. No, of course it isn't your job but since you are home these days I just thought . . . No. No problem. Tell you what: I'll take you out. How's that. A treat. *(No reply.)* No. You're tired. Right. Fine. So. What'll we eat? You're not hungry? I don't care if you're hungry or not, the point is you've got to eat. Not for you, for the baby. No, you're not getting fat. You can diet later – get rid of that. I know: why don't you make scrambled eggs. No? Right, fine. Okay. I'll get some take away. No problem. See: no problem. *(Rolls his eyes.)* Wheeooo! *(Shakes head.)*

SCENE THIRTEEN

All four characters on stage. MOTHER *unscrews bottle top and hands bottle to* WOMAN *who holds the hat in front of her as baby.*

MOTHER Come on, drink up.

WOMAN Can't stand the stuff.

MOTHER For the babe; it's the wine of the gods above.

FRIEND *(Teasing.)* You're just the incubator, my love.

WOMAN *drinks obedient as a child. Hands bottle back to* MOTHER.

MOTHER *(Handing* WOMAN *the bottle again. This time it's a urine sample jar.)* Come on pet; just a little bit.

WOMAN *(Refusing bottle.)* I can't. There's nothing in me.

MAN Just a little piss; for the test.

WOMAN I'll miss.

MAN Come on darling; I'm going to be late. Pull yourself together.

MOTHER Co-operate.

WOMAN *takes bottle, lowers self, perches precariously over it.*

MOTHER There's a good girl.

FRIEND That's the trick.

MAN That's the ticket.

FRIEND . . . all there is to it . . .

MAN Why all the fuss!

WOMAN *struggles up. Knocks over the bottle in her struggle.*

WOMAN Oh no! Oh Shit!

MAN Don't sit on it!

MOTHER *(Grabbing her apron to wipe up.)* No problem. You'll just have to do it again.

WOMAN What a pain.

FRIEND You're not concentrating . . .

MAN I'm not waiting.

MOTHER *(Wiping bottle hands it to* WOMAN.*)* Right now. Come on. One more time.

WOMAN The urine sample assembly line . . . I used to make millions dealing in shares; now I'm passing urine that isn't there.

WOMAN *throws up her hands in despair.*

SCENE FOURTEEN

WOMAN *and* MOTHER *on stage with crate/table.* MOTHER *demonstrates, using her apron as a nappy and the bottle as a baby.*

MOTHER Then this goes here. Then this goes here like this. You try.

WOMAN *tries, with little success.*

MOTHER No, no, no. Don't cry. This comes up here, like this. Then you tuck it in, and pin . . .

WOMAN Yes but . . .

MOTHER No. Not there; on this bit.

WOMAN Yes but . . . it will have legs – won't it?

MOTHER *looks horrified at* WOMAN. WOMAN *shrugs.*

SCENE FIFTEEN

WOMAN *lies on stage propped up against the crate.* FRIEND *visits with flowers.* WOMAN *takes bouquet and lays it beside her, where it becomes the baby.*

FRIEND How did it go? He tells me it wasn't a bad labour.

WOMAN As labours go . . . *(Wry.)* He should know. *(Points to baby/bouquet.)* It's in there.

FRIEND Oh, isn't he sweet. He's a darling. Adorable.

WOMAN He is a she.

MAN *enters with* MOTHER.

MAN Over and out in six hours flat; I told you it would go like that.

MOTHER *picks up and cradles baby.*

MOTHER He has his father's button nose.

FRIEND He has his mother's curly hair.

MOTHER She has her father's gorgeous eyes.

MAN She has her mother's icy stare.

WOMAN *heaves herself up and looks. Takes baby,* MAN *looks on.*

WOMAN She has my eyes.

MAN He has your eyes. She has your ears.

WOMAN He has my nose.

MAN She has your cheeks.

WOMAN He has your lips.

MAN She has your lips.

WOMAN He has my eyes.

MAN He has my eyes.

WOMAN She has your nose.

MAN He has my hair.

WOMAN He must do. I still have mine.

She throws him the baby.

SCENE SIXTEEN

All characters on stage. MAN *holds bottle,* MOTHER *holds baby/bouquet.* WOMAN *and* FRIEND *watch on.*

MAN Can I have him?

MOTHER Can I hold him?

FRIEND Can I touch him?

WOMAN Don't disturb; the baby's sleeping. *(Passes it to* FRIEND.*)*

FRIEND Look. Her eyelids. Do they dream? *(Passes baby to* MAN.*)*

MOTHER You bet!

MAN *(Alarmed.)* Shit! The baby's waking! *(Passes it to* WOMAN.*)*

WOMAN Uggh. The baby's wet. *(Passes it on to* MOTHER.*)*

SCENE SEVENTEEN

All characters on stage. WOMAN *holds baby/bouquet. (This scene hints at a baptism.)*

MAN Can I have . . .

FRIEND Can I hold . . .

MOTHER Can I love . . .

MAN Can I cherish . . .

FRIEND For richer . . .

MOTHER For poorer . . .

MAN In sickness . . .

FRIEND In health . . .

MOTHER From this day forward . . .

MAN For ever and ever . . .

WOMAN *(Wry aside.)* Or at least for the next twenty years . . .

MAN *(Aside.)* God give me wealth.

MOTHER As long as you both shall live.

WOMAN *(Aside.)* God give me stealth.

WOMAN Or at least until it's an adult.

FRIEND I do.

MOTHER I do.

MAN In the name of . . .

WOMAN My father.

MAN My father.

MOTHER His father's name.

WOMAN My mother's name.

FRIEND Your maiden name.

MAN My name. We'll name it after me.

FRIEND His name!? . . . Shame; it's so mundane.

SCENE EIGHTEEN

All characters gather round baby/bouquet.

MAN He'll be a butcher . . .

WOMAN . . . a baker . . .

MAN . . . a candlestick-maker . . .

WOMAN . . . a rich man . . .

MAN . . . a poor man . . .

WOMAN . . . a beggar man . . .

MAN . . . thief.

MOTHER She'll be sugar . . .

FRIEND . . . and spice . . .

MOTHER . . . and everything nice.

MAN He'll be a lawyer, just like me.

WOMAN She'll be a doctor, like I wanted to be.

FRIEND She'll be a beauty, and a charmer too.

MOTHER He'll be a bounder, just like you.

WOMAN She'll be full of grace . . .

MAN . . . fair of face . . .

WOMAN . . . full of woe . . .

MAN . . . with far to go.

WOMAN She'll be loving and giving . . .

MAN . . . work hard for a living.

MOTHER She'll marry a prince and live happily ever after.

FRIEND For ever and ever, amen . . .

WOMAN . . . ah women too.

SCENE NINETEEN

All characters on stage. MAN, MOTHER *and* FRIEND *circle* WOMAN.

MAN I would but . . .

FRIEND I would but . . .

MAN I would but I have to . . .

MOTHER It's a shame; what a pity – this bad leg of mine . . .

FRIEND Sorry love, got a date.

MAN Sorry love, I'll be late.

FRIEND Ring up your mother . . .

MOTHER Another time.

FRIEND Why can't he do it?

MAN I'm busy all week.

FRIEND Heavy schedule; I'm worked off my feet.

MOTHER You know how it is; my back is so sore . . .

FRIEND *(To audience.)* Well, it is her baby. She wanted the thing. I warned her. What does she expect. They're boring, essentially. Babies are boring. Other people's kids are a bore.

Scene Twenty

WOMAN *(Holds up bottle/baby.)* What a bore!

MOTHER *(Grabs baby, cuddles it.)* Pretty baby.

FRIEND Cute kid.

MOTHER Little pet.

MAN Little thing.

MOTHER Little lamb.

FRIEND Little muffin.

MAN Bambino.

MOTHER A cherub.

FRIEND A pudding.

MOTHER A honey.

MAN A sweet'um.

WOMAN Let's eat him.

All look horrified.

Scene Twenty-one

MAN *alone on stage with baby/bouquet. Dandles baby on his lap. Expression changes as he smells. Lifts hand and sniffs it. Feels baby's nappy which is clearly wet. Looks anxiously around. Forced to change nappy himself, becomes quite taken by the idea. Undoes nappy (paper around the bouquet). Sickened by the mess. Retches. Quickly rewraps nappy.*

MAN *(Calls to wings.)* Darling. *(No response, calls louder.)* Darling! *(No response.)* Darling. Honey. Babyface! *(No response.)* Can you come here a minute. Step on it. Race! *(No response. Calls angrily.)* Hey! Darling! This is important.

WOMAN *enters.*

MAN I've forgotten. Show me again. You do it once more; I feel rotten.

MAN *exits.* WOMAN *sighs, unwraps nappy, looks, closes nappy.*

WOMAN *(Shouts.)* Mom. Ma. Mother. Show me again.

MOTHER *enters,* WOMAN *leaves. As* MOTHER *is approaching baby on table, the hat is thrown in from the wings. She becomes* MAN *again.* MAN *unwraps nappy.*

MAN Darling. *(No response.)* Honey! *(No response.)* Can you come here a minute . . .

SCENE TWENTY-TWO

As characters speak, they pass the baby round.

MAN It's your turn.

WOMAN It's your turn.

MOTHER It's my turn.

FRIEND It's her turn.

WOMAN It's my turn.

MAN It's your turn.

WOMAN I'm not doing it now.

All turn once around. WOMAN *hands baby to* MOTHER.

MOTHER *(To* WOMAN.*)* I told you so. (MOTHER *hands baby to* FRIEND.*)*

FRIEND *(To* MOTHER.*)* I told you so. *(Hands baby to* MAN. MAN *hands baby to* WOMAN .*)*

WOMAN *(To* FRIEND.*)* I told you so.

SCENE TWENTY-THREE

MAN *and* WOMAN *lie in bed – i.e. propped against table.* WOMAN *cradles baby.*

MAN Hey. There isn't room for all three of us here. *(*WOMAN *ignores him.)* There isn't room for three in this bed. *(*WOMAN *ignores him.)* There isn't room for me in this bed. *(*WOMAN *ignores him.)* There isn't room for him in this bed. *(*MAN *grabs baby.)*

WOMAN *(Grabs baby.)* There isn't room for her in this bed.

MAN *(Grabs baby.)* There isn't room for me in this bed.

WOMAN *(Grabs baby.)* There isn't room for you in this bed. There's only room for two in this bed.

MAN It should be me and you in this bed.

MAN *attempts to grab baby.* WOMAN *whisks it away from him. He gets out of bed. She shrugs. He leaves.*

WOMAN Now there's just us two in this bed.

SCENE TWENTY-FOUR

MAN *and* WOMAN *on stage.* MAN *has hat and is about to leave.* WOMAN *holds baby.* WOMAN *thrusts baby at* MAN *and grabs his hat. Throughout the scene both tug over hat. Neither relinquishes it so it is passed back and forth.*

WOMAN I need to get out.

MAN I need to get to work.

WOMAN I need to work.

MAN You don't have work.

WOMAN I'll get work.

MAN I need to work till you get work.

WOMAN But I need to get out to get work.

MAN But I need to work because you don't have work.

WOMAN But I need to get out to get work.

MAN But I need to work till you do get work.

WOMAN But I need to get work.

MAN But you don't have work.

WOMAN But I need to work.

MAN I need to get to work.

MAN *passes baby back to* WOMAN. *She relinquishes hat. He leaves.*

WOMAN *(To the empty stage.)* But I need to get out.

SCENE TWENTY-FIVE

All characters on stage. WOMAN *and* MAN *play out beginning of previous scene – i.e.* MAN *dons hat and prepares to leave.* WOMAN *holds baby.* WOMAN *thrusts baby at* MAN, *grabs hat.*

MAN Who's going to mind the baby?

WOMAN You're going to mind the baby.

MAN I'm not going to mind the baby.

MOTHER Who's going to mind the baby?

MAN *(To* WOMAN*)* You're going to mind the baby.

WOMAN I mind the baby. I mind it a lot.

MAN It isn't an it, it's a he.

WOMAN It's a she.

MOTHER It's a she.

FRIEND It's a he.

WOMAN It's an it.

MOTHER He's a pet.

WOMAN She's a dear.

MAN She's a trooper.

FRIEND A fish-face.

MOTHER A cute little tyke.

WOMAN A bunny.

MAN A honey.

MOTHER A wee little mite.

MAN A babe!

WOMAN It's my baby.

MAN *My* baby!

WOMAN You're lying.

FRIEND It's crying.

MOTHER Don't cry Baby.

MAN Don't, cry baby.

WOMAN Don't cry Baby.

Love and Truffles

(Mike Harris)

Interview with the author

Where did the idea come from?

I was working with a youth theatre group I ran for five or six years and the North West Arts Association gave us money to put together a professional show to tour youth clubs. The basic idea came from subsequent improvisations with a small professional company formed from that group.

And it played to youth club audiences?

It played youth clubs, community centres, schools and theatres, and has since been done by two other professional companies. I don't write for specific audiences. Good drama should work with everybody. People like to put theatre in boxes: 'youth theatre', 'theatre in education', 'fringe theatre' – it allows them to stop thinking.

Shakespeare wrote for everybody – which is just about right, I'd say.

What about the title? It was called 'Ada' once, wasn't it?

We called it *'Ada'* because we couldn't think of anything better. When there was a second act commissioned, and it was turned into a full-length piece, the director suggested *Love and Truffles*. I think it's a rotten title myself, but I didn't come up with anything better, so . . .

So what would you call it now?

I've no idea. I haven't thought about it for four years. I suppose I'd still call it *Love and Truffles* because it got some good reviews at the time!

The original version was written in a fairly strong dialect, which some people – especially those who don't come from the north of England, as you do – might find hard.

Yes. And I've not written a play in that way since. But actually, it wasn't dialect. It was a phonetic rendering of colloquial Manchester, and I don't think it gained much by being so.

The rhythms and idioms of popular regional speech can be done without resorting – as this play did – to invented spellings that try to 'read' as accents sound. Better to suggest the accent and let the audience sound it in its head.

Isn't it a pretty pessimistic view of relationships between the sexes?

Yes, but pessimism done with a fair bit of *joie de vivre*. Just look at the mess sex gets most of us into. The second part of *Love and Truffles* [not in this book] is perhaps not so pessimistic. There is hope offered by the quirky relationship that develops between Trevor and Ada.

Are people really as obsessed with sex as they are in this play?

But it's not a play just about sex, is it? It's about the mating game. And there's nothing in the play that the average fourteen year old doesn't talk about and hasn't seen on parents' videos and on television, after the witching hour of nine.

Besides, it's a highly moral play.

Is it?

Yes. But you can decide yourself what the moral is. Don't

try too hard, though because it's a comedy, not a major work of art.

What happened when audiences saw it?

They laughed. A lot of it is what you'd find in the average TV sit-com, except the dialogue's better and, hopefully, there's space left round the characters so they can breathe a little and start to live in the imagination.

Is it a man's play?

I'm a man, and I wrote it, yes.

But the women are the more interesting characters?

It's always more interesting to write people who are not the same as yourself.

But you seem to be more sympathetic to the women than to the men.

Women are nicer than men, by and large. And therefore, how can they help not being more sympathetic?

What actually happens in the sequal – the part we haven't got here?

We go into Mabel's history – her several husbands and the horrible types she's been involved with. We see Des and Carol's relationship continue through engagement, shotgun marriage, and on to a predictable and doomed journey through life. They're stereotyped, of course, but we enjoy seeing it happen, which is what makes it a comedy.

And there's the rather whimsical Trevor and Ada relationship, as they find a way to an acceptance of each other and what they are; and it is suggested at the end that they are beginning to invent their own quirky rules that escape the stereotypes.

But talking too much about a comedy like this is taking a

sledgehammer to crack a nut! It's about an audience laughing and empathising in a creative way. The best place for sermons is in church.

Advertising the play

You work in the publicity department of a theatre. You are determined to get audiences in to see Mike Harris' play. You have managed to get hold of these (genuine) newspaper reviews of an earlier production.

'Love & Truffles'

Etcetera Theatre

Mr Choci's Chocolate Factory, Truffles department, is where Mike Harris's characters toil. Two production-line workers. Mabel and Carol, let rip with fast Mancunian humour at the expense of colleagues and bed partners, Harry and Des – and men in general. On the reverse we see beer-swilling Des and petty tyrant Harry spouting the same sexist rantings against their supposed loved ones. But there's a third couple: Ada, a seemingly backward frump, and not-so-clever Trevor, who are fixed-up by Des (played superbly by Paul Brophy) and girlfriend Carol (Helen Higgins). Harris's play is fast, funny and critical without awkward sermonising. Nicola White as Ada is brilliant in a complicated role that combines comic stooge dialogue with bursts of philosophical invective, although disappointingly, Mike Pacey (the play's skilful Director) as Trevor is too camp and coy to be engaging. Anne Harries (Mabel) as the know-it-all older woman, seems ill-at-ease with her Manchester accent and worse, her lines, meaning jokes, were lost. Yet this didn't spoil a play with razor-sharp humour and occasional tenderness used to discover whether 'Girls just wanna have fun'.
Andrew Tuck

Time Out Critics Choice
Love and Truffles
6/4/89

Love is a sweet thing

LOVE AND TRUFFLES (Etcetera Theatre Club)

Mike Pacey et al from the Crumpet Theatre Co. have put on a deliciously funny production with *Love and Truffles*. Writer Mike Harris has created a sharp, wholesome play concerning that most contentious of subjects; courtship and conquest between the sexes.

It is set in a northern chocolate factory where the game of courtship is played out with accompanying stereotypes and rituals, as exemplified by the young Carol and Des, or the older Mabel's candid story of rather ugly relationships, from which she has learnt nothing.

The unlikely, but believable central couple, Ada and Trevor, at first incongruous in the setting of these traditional 'norms', ultimately end with a much more honest and satisfying relationship; partly due to Trevor's complete ignorance on the subject, but mainly due to Ada's almost wilful disregard of the rules. Ada's uncompromising stance is the extreme yardstick against which the accepted behaviour of the others is held up for satirical judgement. Mike Harris' exploration of the natural logic of Ada, who refuses to make small-talk simply to fill silence, or make any concessions to her feelings towards Trevor, against the unthinking subservience to familiar roles that the rest follow slavishly makes irresistable watching.

The vehicle provides many moments of sheer farce as each sex displays their best, or worst traits in well worn cliches. The cast is excellent and the production both fast and moving and slickly entertaining, with the definitive view of sex as "you don't have to be clever to do that, I've seen my gerbils do it." (See Fringe.) HENRY GIBBS

What's On and Where to Go in London
Love and Truffles
6/4/89

□ □ □

LOVE AND TRUFFLES
Crumpet Theatre Company

MIKE HARRIS'S comedy takes a very pessimistic view of sexual relationships, yet everyone in the chocolate factory where it is set seems to be obsessed with them.

Only fat Ada and Trevor the idiot do not have one, until their workmates amuse themselves by bringing them together. It then emerges that Ada is not as stupid as she seems. This play, however is.

It lacks any sense of structure, with one character parading her former husbands on stage for no apparent reason.

The humour is of the most basic variety, and the whole thing is irredeemably vulgar.

One wishes that the actors' skill at lively characterisation had been put to better use than it is at Buster Brown's.

□ □ □

The Scotsman
Love and Truffles
9/88

GW Theatre's *Love And Truffles* is at Liverpool's Neptune Theatre, which is usually the haunt of troupes like the Bootle Amateur Wagner ensemble. The production looks like the earnest Agitprop of the last decade, with a row of women factory workers packing chocolate truffles on a set which consists of three grey folding chairs.

But there's not a word about the struggle for emancipation of the working class; shop floor politics in this place are about who gets off with whom. Plain quiet Ada, played by Lorraine Hackett, is set up by her workmates for the game of life and love with Trevor, the works' simpleton, who is played with sympathy by Dave Jones. Her mentor is the glamorous, worldly wise Carol who falls for every trap with tragic foreknowledge of what and where each trap is, notably archetypal egomaniac Des, played energetically by Brian Morgan.

Mabel, a bit after the Wife of Bath, has already fallen three times and is shamefacedly determined to go over the top again. Ada had hidden depths, she believes you shouldn't talk unless you have something to say, and hers and Trevor's simplicity triumphs over the aborted cynicism of their workmates.

The Independent
Love and Truffles
1989

• Choose the *one word* from all the reviews which could be displayed in huge letters on the side of the theatre, in order to draw the audiences in (e.g. 'VULGAR' – *The Scotsman).*

• Select one sentence from each review that could attract audiences to the new production of *Love and Truffles.*

• Choose ten phrases – or groups of words – from the press articles which would most excite a possible audience, if printed boldly outside the theatre under the headline 'What the papers said'.
For example:

> What the Papers Said:
> '. . .candid story . . . moments of sheer farce . . . the cast is excellent . . .razor-sharp humour . . . vulgar . . .'

For your own private reason (e.g. jealousy, tax evasion) you want audiences to stay away from the coming production, so now:

• Choose the ten phrases – or groups of word – that would most keep an audience at home, under the headline 'What the Papers Said'.

For example:

> What the Papers Said:
> '. . .ugly relationships . . . well-worn cliches . . . ill-at-ease . . . irredeemably vulgar. . . like the Bootle Amateur Wagner ensemble . . .'

Mike Harris says in the interview, 'I think it's a rotten title myself'. What do you think?

• Choose another title – you have five minutes before the posters get printed!

Reading the play

The playwright originally wrote this play using what he called his own 'phonetic rendering of colloquial Manchester'. Here are two examples of the original version of the play:

DES Aye well, yer not as daft as yer crack out to be, are yer? A mean all the stuff yer nick from the factory, Trev. Where've yer stashed it? *(Rummages through boxes.)* Aye, aye. What 'ave we 'ere then? *(Pulls out a box of chocs.)* A one-pound box of Mr Chocky's Chocolate Truffles. Like 'um, do yer, Trevor? Naughty but nice, eh? I imagine yer'll 'av bought these, won't yer? *(Pops one.)*

TREVOR Yer, that's right.

DES *(Spits it out.)* Muck. Only fit fer givin' 'ter bints when yer'v fergot birthdays. What else 'av yer got stashed away? *(Rummages. Stops. Looks at* TREVOR.*)* What's this then? *(Feels.)* You little bleeder. *(Pulls out a handful of sink plugs on chains.)* Wi'v bin stuffin' sink 'oles wi' bog paper for weeks 'cos er you. What you want bloody plugs for?

(from Scene Two)

DES Cos a'm askin' yer to. Please.

CAROL Get stuffed. *(Turns, takes a step or two away, stops, turns back.)* What der yer think I am, eh? What? Nowt? Shit? A'm a person, right – see? A don't need yer, a can live without yer. A'v yer seen me mam? What she's like? Eh, a'v yer? Well a'm not goin' ter be like 'er. A'm not wastin' me life on a bloody fella – fetchin' an carryin' and puttin' up with yer soddin' vomit of a Saturday night – a'm buggered if a'm doin' that – so yer can piss off for me – yer can piss off! *(Turns, steps away.)*

(from Scene Nine)

When the editor decided to include the play in this series, he and the publisher wondered whether students and pupils would be able to understand what was going on, particularly if they did not come from the North West of England.

Eventually they decided that once the words were read out loud for a few pages, the 'code' would be easily 'cracked' – rather more easily, say, than Shakespeare, who is virtually unintelligible for many students at first. They also argued that if the students thought of a soap opera or television series that was set in the same landscape and compared this play with that – well the language would soon be easy.

The playwright was not convinced. He thought his own phonetic rendering in the play was not sufficiently well worked out. As a result he had not written the play in a clearly recognisable dialect, and he felt this would make it difficult even for people in the Manchester area to understand, let alone anyone from elsewhere!

As you can see, the editor and publisher agreed for the play to be published as the playwright wanted, and the play you have just read has been adapted from the original and presented in a 'standardised' language: the versions of the two extracts quoted above, for example, can be found on pages 11 and 33.

- Write a letter to the educational publisher and say whether or not you agree with the decision to rewrite the play in this form. Do you think the play will have lost anything in 'translation'? Do you think it is more important for the play to be understood by as many people as possible or for it to present an accurate reflection of the characters it deals with?

- The play is, even now, written in a very colloquial style. Choose any page and 'translate' it into more formal English, as might be written by educational publishers. (Exaggerate, if it makes more fun!)

For example, here is a 'translation' of the passage we have already seen on page 33:

DES Because I am requesting you to. Please?

CAROL I'm sorry, but who exactly do you imagine I am? A zero? Less than a zero? Well, actually, I am a person. I do not require you; I can exist without you. Have you, I wonder, ever seen Mama? Have you observed what she is like at all? Well, let me inform you that I do not intend to resemble her. I am not wasting my life on a man – doing all the domestic labour. Oh no, I'm very sorry but no way is this person going to do that, so frankly you can boil your head. Just boil same . . .

Exploring the text

• Discuss, in sixes – with someone taking notes to report back to the whole group – 'This play is held together by three love stories. We keep listening for the oldest of reasons: to find out whether the girl will get the boy/boy will get the girl.
– We hope not in the case of Carol.
– We want Mabel to do whatever helps make her happy.
– But, most of all, we want Ada and Trevor to live (together) happily ever after.'

Do you agree?

Which story do you find most interesting? Where are the surprises in the different lovers' relationships?

Do you think people (adult, or not; men, or not) are as 'obsessed with sex' as they are in this play?

• Discuss what you would tell each character if you met them privately.

The *Scotsman* newspaper says that *Love and Truffles* 'lacks any sense of structure'. Do you agree?

• Untangle the structure of the play. Think about how it is put together.

How has Mike Harris chosen to tell his story? How many scenes are there? Where and when are they set? What length are they? Do they start and stop shapelessly? Is every scene 'naturalistic' (i.e. like 'real life', or like a soap opera on television)? Are there theatrical tricks? Are there shapes to the whole play? Or to scenes themselves?

What does 'a sense of structure' mean? What films or plays that you know would you say have a sense of structure? How is this shown?

- Using a diagram, graph, map or drawing, show how the play is put together.

For example, here is a diagram to represent the structure of the pantomime, *Cinderella:*

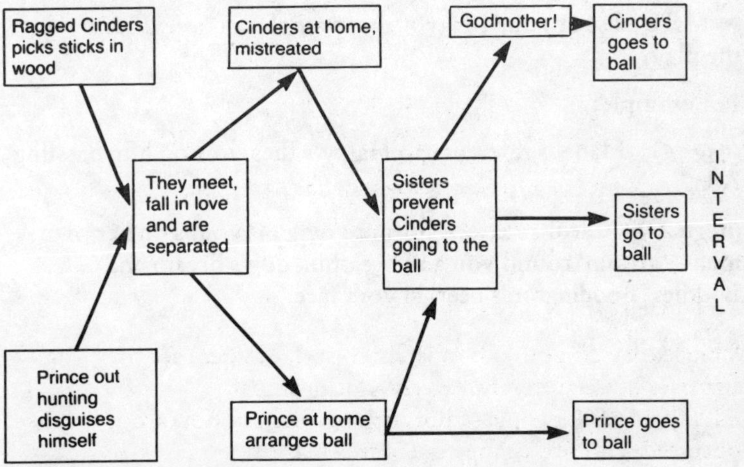

'Pessimism done with a fair bit of *joie de vivre*' is how Mike Harris describes the view of the relationships between the sexes in this play. How pessimistic do you think the play is about men and women?

- In pairs, argue the case.

For example:

ONE It is very pessimistic because it's all sex and no love.

TWO There is love. Ada and Trevor are falling in love by the end of the play; and they won't end up like Carol and Des.

ONE The men are filthy-minded, insensitive and stupid.

TWO The women aren't.

ONE They aren't quite as bad, but they fall for the man, and choose to stay with them.

TWO You look up 'pessimistic' in the dictionary, then, and you'll find . . .

What do you understand by *'joie de vivre'?* How much of it do you think there is in the play?

• Make a list of your 10 favourite examples of *'joie de vivre'* in the play.

For example:

(page 4) Mabel's reference to Harry's flies, to stop him hassling Ada.

(page 29) Carol's reasons for not going into pubs on her own – men – 'gropin' round you and breathin' dog's breath and Boddies [Boddington's beer] in your face.'

And so on.

Designing the play

The director wants this production of *Love and Truffles* to be fresh and new. Ignoring anything said by the playwright either in his play or in his interview, you have to design a dazzling new production for a brand new version, in which 'everything but the kitchen sink' can be used.

• In pairs, discuss and design this new production. Think of other live shows you've seen – like light shows, puppet shows, laser displays and circuses, as well as other plays – and use any ideas from these that might help.

Start with the scenery – do you want scenery? If you do, should it be lifelike or not? How big should it be, and should it be on one level or more? What should it be made of, and what colours do you want it to be? Should you dress up the rest of the theatre as well?

Then think about other effects. Would photographs, slides or collages work? Do you want to use any machinery? If you want props, what should they be like? Do you want to use incidental music, or play tricks with the costumes?

Don't just take the first idea that comes; make this production extraordinary.

- Report back to the rest of the group.

Looking at the characters

The characters are 'typical and familiar . . . but it does not matter, because the play is explicitly about cliché and stereotype'. *The Festival Times.*

The playwright himself says 'A lot of it is what you'd find in the average TV sit-com.' How typical and familiar do you think the characters are? Are all of them clichéd? Do you think some are more clichéd than others?

The director of a new production of *Love and Truffles* decides to do a workshop with the actors, trying to take the production beyond the tempting, clichéd stereotypes.

She writes a short speech of four paragraphs to start the workshop.

- Write her short speech, each paragraph beginning as below.

Para 1

At first sight the characters might seem mere clichés and stereotypes. There's a fat, unattractive woman, who has no love life and is mocked about sex; there's a . . .

Para 2

But, in fact, the characters are more interesting than that. Most interesting of all is perhaps . . .

Para 3

Even the most clichéd, predictable, stereotyped character in the play – probably ____________, can surprise us, as when . . .

Para 4

The audience must not go away from the production thinking they have seen it all before; the six characters must be more than stereotypes. To ensure this, I suggest that in rehearsal we work . . .

• In pairs, find five sentences spoken by each character in that play that show that they are *not* entirely stereotypical or clichéd.

For example: Carol.

> ''Ave you seen me mam? What she's like? Eh, 'ave you? Well, I'm not goin' to be like her.'
>
> ''Cos they don't like brainy women, 'cos it makes 'em realise how thick they are. Better just listen to 'em – it's borin' for you, but they like it a lot.'

And so on.

• Choose any one character from the play. Reread all the speeches made by that character, and any reference to her/him that the others make.

Your chosen character has been described in a newspaper as a 'stereotype'. Your character replies to this accusation in a two-page letter.

For example:

> 'So, you think I'm a stereotype, do you? All right, let me tell you this about me, then – bet you didn't know it. I worked in that sweet factory all right, but you know what I did before, do you? I'll tell you. And I'll tell you this, too . . .'

And the letter could end:

'. . . and that's why I'm not a stereotype and a cliché, right?

Yours sincerely, [etc.]

Mike Harris says that he loves all the characters in this play, and 'if you like your characters and can also criticise them, then you're half-way there.'

- Find a speech, or an action, from the play for each character that seems best to show that the playwright loves her/him.

- In one sentence of your own, say what you think the playwright thinks of the characters, and what he 'criticises' them for.

- The director says he thinks the workshop has been very helpful. He asks you to go away and search magazines for faces, or sketch/draw/paint your own, that would suit the characters in the play.

- Write a poem called 'Love and Truffles' about the people in the play.

After the curtain is down

Was it a 'man's play'?

Mike Harris answers the question in the interview by saying, 'I'm a man and I wrote it, yes.' Was it a silly question?

Or is there another suggestion behind it – developed in the following question – a suggestion that it's the kind of play a man *would* write, however sympathetic to women?

Do you think men *can* write realistically about women? Or women about men? How can each gender know exactly how the other thinks or feels?

Do you think Mike Harris is less kind to his men than to his women? Does he present them as more stupid/selfish/weak/ ridiculous than the women?

And is it odd that it is one of the women, Ada, who seems to be expressing the views of the author?

- Write a two-page account beginning, 'If a female playwright had written *Love and Truffles*, I think she . . .'

In the theatre bar, after the show, a group of four or five people sit discussing Mike Harris' description of his play in the programme. They are especially interested that he says, 'There's nothing in the play that the average 14 year old doesn't talk about and hasn't seen on parents' videos and on television after the witching hour of nine. Besides, it's a highly moral play'.

How much of this do you agree with?

Trappin'

(Frances McNeil)

Interview with the author

Why is the play called Trappin'?

The M6 Theatre Company is based in Rochdale, where the word 'trappin' is local slang, meaning to get a boyfriend or a girlfriend. It's such a significant word, it was too good to miss!

Where did the idea for the play come from?

The M6 Company discussed subject areas that they thought were important. The women in the company – two, in particular – had an interest in the issue of male violence towards women. They looked for an existing script, but did not find one they wanted to do. So, they decided to commission a new one. I got a phone call from Maggie Tagney, whom I'd worked with before, and a copy of the brief.

I wanted to do it from the start. I went to see them, and met the management team: Eileen Murphy, Director: Dot Wood, schools liaison officer; Dee Sidwell, designer; Maggie Tagney, actor; and Janet Mathewman, administrator. We talked about my work – they'd read some of my scripts. We discussed the subjects and tried to find out if we were on the same wavelength.

Why was the subject so important?

It's something that many of us come into contact with,

either directly or indirectly. It's difficult to know what to do about something once you are very close to it, or deeply enmeshed. By exploring situations through the play there's a chance to be a little more prepared if the real thing comes along. There are many stereotypes and clichés around on this subject; the drunken husband, the pathetic working-class wife, and the newer clichés where the victim conspires in her own demise. There's a grain of truth in these or they wouldn't last, but they do get in the way of reality much of the time.

The play is only part of what happens in front of an audience?

Yes. It is followed by a forum workshop based on techniques evolved by the Brazilian writer-director Augusto Boal. One tenet of his 'theatre of the oppressed' is that the oppressor will never willingly relinquish power, and in this play Garry is the oppressor.

In the workshop the audience are encouraged to look for moments, for turning points, where change might happen, and they are invited to role-play those moments.

So the audience actually take part in the play?

First the play is performed. Then the audience are asked for the key moments: the first time things begin to go wrong, say. They're invited to get up and see how they themselves might handle the moment differently. In this play it was Viv's part that the audience took – boys as well as girls – because Viv is the oppressed person and ultimately has to find a way out.

And what happened?

The first time we tried the workshop at the teachers' preview, a teacher got up to play Viv and she got so incensed that she hit Garry. Jim Byrne, who played Garry, is such a gentle person and we were all upset. So was the teacher when she got over her anger with Garry and realised she'd hit Jim. After that the workshop leader always made the point of saying, 'No violence. If you feel like hitting Garry, freeze.'

Someone would make a suggestion, get up and put it into action, and then find that the situation was much harder to change than they imagined.

Do Viv and Garry love each other?

Ah now . . . that's a question I'd like people to ask themselves. I don't want to say what I think. In the play Garry says 'I love you'. But what does he mean? What is he doing when he says it?

We don't hear Viv say the words. I couldn't write those words for her. But it doesn't mean they aren't there. Perhaps more pointedly there if they're not spoken?

You mentioned the idea of the 'victim'. How far do you think Viv is to blame for what happens to her?

Not at all. It's not her fault. Violence against women is the only crime in which the behaviour of the victim and the aggressor are linked. You wouldn't ask the question if it was a mugging or a murder. There's the assumption that domination is legal if it's motivated by love. It's not.

Where did Jane come from?

I wanted characters that contrasted in each of the couples. Garry wants to be up and doing and so does Jane, yet Garry calls Jane 'aggressive'. Laurie and Jane have their differences, but they sort them out without her bopping him over the head or vice versa. I'm interested in friendship because I think it's important – friendship can help us survive.

Do you think the play is less sympathetic to men than to women?

Well, with the Laurie character I did want someone who is very sorted out and knows his own mind – who is quite a strong person but would never be violent. I'm not unsympathetic to Garry's conscious desires: he works hard, he wants a nice home – why not? I wasn't interested in making a moral judgement on his personality. It's his unconscious desires that cause the problems. This was too short a piece to deal with that. The point is, we live in a society that produces and nurtures people like Garry.

What set was used to act the play on?

There were large photographs of Viv as a baby with her mum, Viv and Jane, Viv working in the office – and the wedding photo. At key moments in the play the photos, one by one, had a blind fall over them – as bits of her life slipped away from her, till she was only left with the wedding.

The room was a square with a skirting board, and the skirting board had entrances and exits. As the play progressed they were closed – until there was no way out.

At one stage in planning the play you intended to include Viv's diary as part of the action. Why did you drop it?

The diary carried too much; the passage of time, inner thoughts, descriptions of the violence done. Also it was too literary – it held up the action. Everybody had to stand still while she stood and said it.

I wanted the play to keep moving, to have action and movement – particularly because it was aimed primarily at fifteen and sixteen year olds. I wanted things to keep happening. Had it been a longer play – it was meant to last 45 minutes and in fact lasted 55 – it would not have been so uneven to have the diary.

What advice do you have for students working on the play?

Go for the characters, go for the story and then see. If you want some key words to bear in mind, these were jotted down before I started writing: devaluation, subordination, isolation and humiliation.

How did the audiences react to the play and the forum method, which involved them in being part of the theatre they saw?

Young people just starting out in a relationship were already identifying with some of the patterns they saw in the relationships in the play. Some women from a Refuge came to see it – and one woman sat on the front row and just cried. The play spoke to people of different ages and experiences. People did get up to participate in the role play, and would begin confidently and then find that their strategy didn't work. The situation is difficult, not at all simple to solve.

The play doesn't end, does it?

No. The last part would be a very unsatisfactory ending if it was just a play; but it was deliberately a question mark. Immediately the play ends – or doesn't – the workshop leader talks to the audience and says something like, 'That's how it stands at the moment, what should happen now?' People offer ideas, and then they take a five-minute break and come back, and everything opens out in the discussion of the key moments, the turning points – and someone is invited to role-play Viv, and see how things could be different.

Do you yourself know how the story ends?

Yes. I think I do. But I don't know if I should say.

Advertising the play

'*Trappin*' is a brilliant title when you live in Rochdale,' says the marketing director of the theatre. 'But no one knows what it means anywhere else. Get in a huddle and find me a new title, only I need it in fifteen minutes.'

- Get in a huddle and rename the play, in fifteen minutes.

Some writers say titles are the hardest things they ever have to make up. Try:

using some other local slang, dialect or idiom.
scanning the play for words of groups of words to use as the title for the complete work. (It's a trick used to name the books in this *Upstage* series.)
using a well-known phrase or saying.
writing a list as fast as you can think it ('brainstorming').

- Using your new title, design the poster. (You will probably have to include something about the 'forum' method – see Frances McNeil's notes on this in answering the fourth question above.)

Designing the play

Frances McNeil explains the set used in the original Rochdale production, which seemed to work very well. You are eager to use it for your own production, but your version is being performed 'in the round' (with the audience on all four sides) and the photographs don't work.

- Discuss this snag, and how to solve the design problem for your production.
- Do the rough drawings for a new design.

Casting

- Cast the play using actors you know from TV.
- Have a meeting to discuss your castings. How far should you

'cast to type' (making heroes handsome, lovers beautiful, etc.), and how far *against* type?

- Cast the play.

- Collectively decide on the best cast you can find in the world for your production of *Trappin'*.

The agent for the actor who has been offered the part of Mrs Benson (Viv's mum) rings up to say her client has to have more to do in the show or she won't accept the job. The agent is reassured that there are some new scenes on the way, featuring the character much more . . .

- Write the synopsis for two more scenes featuring Mrs Benson.

- Make three suggestions for more things the character can do or say in the scenes where she already appears in the play.

- Invent another character altogether who can 'double' with Mrs Benson – i.e. the actor playing Mrs Benson can play this new character when Mrs Benson is not on stage. For example, the new character could be a window cleaner at Viv's flat window.

- Write a letter to the agent, outlining the improvement in the part offered to the actor.

Exploring the text

The director thinks rehearsals have got stodgy, and new energy is needed. You have to play a rehearsal game.

- Read several consecutive pages of the play, in groups of four.

- Find a space, and place the four characters in it – not according to where they are in 'real life' but according to how well they are or not getting on with each other.

For example, you might feel that at the start of your chosen section Garry and Viv are very close, Jane is a little excluded, Mrs Benson is almost forgotten and Laurie doesn't even exist. The chosen placings might look like this:

Garry Viv

Jane Mrs Benson

• Very slowly read your chosen pages. Each character should move nearer to or further away from the other characters according to how he/she *feels about what he/she is saying, or what is being said.*

For example, a little later in the play than the above set-up, the pattern might be like this:

Garry Viv

Laurie Jane Mrs Benson

The M6 Theatre Company, who asked Frances McNeil to write this play for them, compiled a 'pack' about the play and the issues around it. This was meant for students to work on before or after the play and the discussions that followed it in the 'forum' way.

Among the 'questions and activities relating directly to the play' was this:

Consider times in the play when the power balance between the two characters was as below:

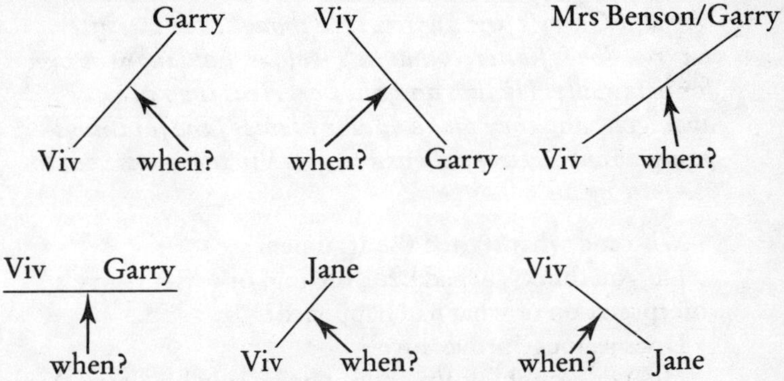

Discuss what actions, words or physical contact was happening at these points. What were the different ways in which characters in the play had power over someone else?

Reconstruct some of those powerful/powerless images (image 1). Change the image into something more equal (image 2). With improvised dialogue, move the last image to the second.

How difficult was it?

How did the actors in the image(s) feel?

Look at a selection of pictures in colour supplements or adverts – discuss who is in the powerful position in each.

When in the play were Garry and Viv close/far apart?

When in the play were Viv and Jane close/far apart?

What factors affect the power balance between Garry and Viv?

- Can you make useful sense of this?
- Work through the suggestions, and see how they illuminate the play and its themes.

Also in the pack was a scene-by-scene summary of what happens in the play, and some questions.

Here is a summary for scene 3:

3) Flat – twenty minutes later.

Viv and Garry's first big row. He thought she was after Laurie. She is flattered that he's jealous, but laughs at him for being silly. He flips and hits her. He is then very apologetic and they make up. He blames Jane for things going wrong between them and gets Viv to promise not to see Jane again.

Who and what started the argument?

Do you think Viv had been flirting, or was it Garry's interpretation of what had happened?

Does jealousy prove 'love'?

How do you think Viv feels at being told by Garry 'You were acting like a whore'?

How does Garry want Viv to behave at parties?

What do you think each of them was thinking or feeling immediately after the hit?

What methods or tactics does Garry use to shift the blame and to get Viv to agree to stop seeing Jane?

Did Viv really want to give up seeing Jane? If not, why has she agreed to it?

GARRY I couldn't bear to see you dancing with him. I wouldn't have hit you if I didn't love you so much. Do you believe me?

VIV I think so.

GARRY Think so? You know so. I panic at the thought that something will go wrong for us.

What is Garry's idea of things going right or wrong for them?

Does hitting someone prove you love them?

Why is it important to Garry that Viv and Jane's friendship ends?

- Check that the summary is an accurate version of scene 3.

- In groups, answer the questions.
  Are there other questions that might be interesting to ask? And answer?

- Read and summarise another scene.

- Write up the questions you think would get a useful discussion started.

- Swap scenes with other groups. Again, check their summary, answer their questions and consider what other questions might be worth asking.

The pack also included a section of 'unhelpful myths and stereotypes about domestic violence, with some comments about what really happens'. Among them were these:

> It's just the odd domestic tiff . . . it can't be that bad or she'd leave.
> No-one should interfere in the domestic affairs of man and wife.
> Domestic violence only happens in working-class or problem families.
> She must ask for it.
> It's only drunks or macho men who beat their wives.
> They must come from violent backgrounds.
> Abused women tend to abuse their children.
> She's not really threatened with violence. It's just an excuse to get rehoused.

> The pack also includes the number of the National Women's Aid helpline – 0272-428368. They might be able to help in your work.

- In pairs, spend about three minutes arguing about one of these stereotypes – in role.

For example:

ONE Of course she asks for it. If she didn't, she'd leave.

TWO And have nowhere to live.

ONE She could go to the housing. Anyway, if she didn't annoy him he'd not hit her.

TWO So she likes being hit?

ONE Some people . . .

• Report back to the whole group on how the argument went. How easy it is to decide the real truth about the 'stereotypes'? What kind of 'evidence' was there? What 'anecdotal evidence' (stories people knew from real life) come out? What further evidence would be needed to prove/disprove the 'stereotypes'? How might you find it? (The pack includes some suggested responses by the Women's Aid organisation – for example, is it possible to say 'no-one should interfere in the domestic affairs of man and wife' when 25 per cent of reported violent crime is wife assault?)

• Together, compile a list of unhelpful myths and stereotypes about some related matter.

For example:

unhelpful myths and stereotypes about marriage
unhelpful myths about love
unhelpful myths and stereotypes about men and women
unhelpful myths about men.

Rehearsing the play

Frances McNeil briefly outlines the writer-director Augustus Boal's idea of the 'theatre of the oppressed' in her answer to the fifth and sixth questions in the interview above.

The director decides to try the theatre-of-the-oppressed forum techniques in rehearsal, and gives out these instructions:

- Search out a moment in Viv's story when she makes a crucial decision of some kind that changes (or does not change) what could happen next.

These moments do not need to be massively dramatic. You might, for example, find that a remark like 'Well, maybe not' (page 52, line 9) is really crucial to what happens afterwards – doesn't Viv know that Garry is wrong about women who do self-defence? After all, her friend is into it. If she had persisted in the idea of learning to defend herself, might things have been different?

Another key moment might be when she says: 'You're crazy. I've never looked at anyone else since I met you' (page 56, line 21) – just after his first really violent act. What if she had said something different at this moment of change, like 'That's the first and last time you ever hit me and I'm . . .'?

Or what about her answer to Garry when he says 'Stop seeing her' (page 58, line 7)?

- In role play, or in a written form, or both, use the theatre of the oppressed/forum technique on your chosen moment. See what happens when Viv 'handles the moment differently'.

Is the outcome different? How easy *is* it to change things?

- Find the most interesting moment in *each scene* between Garry and Viv and try 'handling the moment differently'.

Looking at the characters

Viv

Viv's diary was one part of the play Frances McNeil originally wrote but subsequently dropped (see the twelfth question in the interview above).

The director decides the diary idea might help the actors discover more about Viv in rehearsal. You are asked to:

- Write up what Viv put in her diary on seven key dates in her life:

  the night she met Garry
  the night before she got married
  very late on New Year's Eve (year 1)
  in the July of year 2
  June in year 3
  April in year 5
  New Year's Eve in year 6 (or seven, or eight, twenty years later)

What do you know of Viv from the play? For example, what was her home life like before her marriage? What are her mother and father like? What kind of school career did she have? What were her other boyfriends and her other friendships like? What ambitions did she have?

- Put Viv in the 'hot seat' and quiz her about herself. 'Viv' will have to invent what the play doesn't tell her.

Does Viv love Garry? Frances McNeil says 'I couldn't write those words for her'. Why not?

- Report Viv's thoughts about Garry – as a poem or a song, or as a 'stream of consciousness' (her thoughts just as they come out), or as a (love) letter, or maybe as a picture.

The M6 pack warns about 'Unhelpful myths and stereotypes about domestic violence'. But how 'stereotyped' is Viv herself? (i.e. what does she do that might be 'typical' of wives who are battered? What does she do that is not 'typical'?)

How far is what happened her fault? (And do you agree with Frances McNeil, who invented her?) Is she too weak? *Does* she invite what happens?

Garry makes a statement to the police, investigating an incident of alleged domestic violence.

- Improvise the scene, in groups.

- Write up the policeman's account of Garry's version of the marriage.

Garry

The playwright doesn't think her play is 'less sympathetic' to men than to women. Do you agree?

The actor playing Garry thinks he is too unsympathetic, and will be hard for him to play convincingly – 'He's just a baddie'. The director understands the problem and suggests some work to help the actor.

- Reread all Garry's speeches in order.

- Try reading out some of his dialogue 'against the text' – so that even though the words might suggest one attitude, the actor tries to make them mean something else.

(For example, Garry could be acted in a way that is more charming than the words might at first suggest; or more humorous, gentle, likeable, happy, or quiet.)

Does this playing 'against the text' help?

A visitor calls to have a word with Garry about what is going on in his home. The visitor could be the doctor, Mrs Benson, a priest, a neighbour or a marriage guidance advisor, for example.

- Create the dialogue.

Does Garry have to lie to explain what is happening? Or does what he is doing make sense from his point-of-view? Is he ashamed? Is he bad?

Is there something 'wrong' with Garry? Would he have been the same with whoever he had married? Does he 'love' Viv? (The playwright says that when Garry says 'I love you' you have to ask what he actually means. And what is he doing at the time he says it?)

- Make two lists:

  evidence that Garry loves his wife
  evidence that he doesn't.

Jane and Laurie

- Reread their lines.
- Create some missing scenes in their relationship.

For example:

their first meeting
the time they decide they will marry/live together
a discussion about whether they will have children
a discussion about whether they ought to interfere in what's happening to her friend Viv
an argument they have that isn't resolved in 'bopping' (however strong she is).

Suppose Garry married Jane and Laurie married Viv.

- Write the scene-by-scene synopsis of *that* play.

Doctor

The director decides the doctor's part is too small and dull for the actor who will be playing it for the next several months. The director asks for your help in making the part more interesting, for the actor and/or audience.

- Reread everything the doctor says.
- 'Hot seat' her/him, making her/him extremely special.
- Rewrite her/his speeches so that they still fit the story of the play but she/he now says twice as much, and makes a more interesting contribution to the play.

• Discuss whether your character is better than the one Frances McNeil created. Does the character help the play? Do there always have to be some bit-part players – in plays and in real life?

After the curtain is down

So successful is the production that the theatre manager insists on a sequel.

• Create the scenario for *'Trappin' 2'* (just when you thought it was safe to speak to a man.)

For example:

> *At* GARRY'S *funeral, year 7.*
> LAURIE *comes, greets* VIV, *says* JANE *is about to have a baby, asks . . .*

Frances McNeil says that the M6 Theatre Company 'had an interest in the issue of male violence towards women' and looked for a script but couldn't find one. Yet many other people *have* written about such matters – including Shakespeare.

• What poems, stories, plays, films, videos and articles can you collect together, or in other ways bring in as evidence?

For example:

> Shakespeare's *Othello* is a play about wife murder.
> Tracy Chapman's song 'Behind the Wall' (which begins 'Last night I heard the screaming') is on the same themes – and was used in the M6 Company production during scene changes.
>
> And of course there's the classic wife-beating play *'Punch and Judy'*.

• Together recall and write the scenario for the classic *'Punch and Judy.'*

For example:

> *Scene One – Outside the Punch household*
> *Mr Punch enters with stick and explains to his dog Toby what a clever Punch he is, and how he likes sausages and . . .*

How similar is Judy's story to Viv's? How different are they?

- Try the theatre of the oppressed/forum technique on *Punch and Judy*', looking for the moments the oppressed Judy could have handled differently, and so perhaps saved herself.

Frances McNeil says 'by exploring situations through the play there is a chance to be a little more prepared if the real thing comes along'.

- Do you feel any more 'prepared' for the 'real thing' if it happens to you or people you know?

- What have you learned in exploring this play and related matters?

- Have your views changed? Has your behaviour changed at all? Will either change?

The playwright says that young people like you, 'just starting in a relationship, were already identifying with some of the patterns they saw in the relationships in the play'.

- Do you?

- Make a list for the *Daily Tabloid* of 'twenty-one ways you didn't know to stop wife battering'.

The playwright suggests four words to think of when working on her play:

devaluation
subordination
isolation
humiliation.

- Think of them, and round them. What experiences in your own life would suggest each of those words most?

- Write a play, poem, story or article suggested by one of these words:

  devalued
  subordinated
  isolated
  humiliated.

Don't Cry Baby
(Katie Campbell)

Interview with the author

Where did the idea come from?

I was 30 myself and in that situation. Should I have a child? Shouldn't I? My partner was anxious to have a child and in principle so was I. But there was my career. I'm not very maternal but I like the idea.

Watching all my friends have children, I was aware of the strain. They all seemed to be brain-damaged by it, for the first two years at least.

It's a problem couples face now that they didn't in the past so much. There is no longer that assumption that you *will* have children. Now there is a choice.

How did the play come about?

It's all the arguments in your head, all the pressures – all the various characters.

It's one of those issues everyone feels they have a right to get in on. But you can have the same conversation on different days and people will say different things – the mother might say something one day and then the opposite the next. I wanted the play to express that – how if you get a girlfriend on a good day she'll say, 'Go ahead have a child', and on the next day she'll say, 'Don't do it.' It's an emotional issue – which is why the play is told in an emotional rather than a straightforward way.

I hope this doesn't sound too pompous – but deciding whether or not to have a child strikes one of the deepest human chords – the desire to procreate and the problems that come with it.

Some people find the play difficult – even to understand what's going on.

I don't think it matters. I don't mind. There is a constant stream of repeats. And it's complicated because the issues are complicated. The characters are universal – they are almost anonymous.

And the icons? What's the idea of them?

I wanted the play to be very gymnastic, like child's play or a circus – a bit of a game, with an element of mime as well, universality and cartoon. I wanted it visually stimulating and quick. And I wanted the audience to see the point of view from the icon.

There are four stock characters; the icon indicates who is which at any moment in the play. It could be done without the icons but I like the idea of responsibility being thrown around with the icons – for example, throwing the baby about – it suggests how selfish and callous people can be.

Does the play have to be performed by three women and one man?

It can be done by four women or four men, or any combination. The emotions expressed are not gender-specific. You often get men who resist having children as much as women do. Or men who have the urge to have children, and it's the women who resist . . . in fact, I think men nowadays are taking the more feminine line and getting broody – more often it's the women who are resisting and saying, 'Wait a minute, what about *my* life, *my* career?'

Could it be performed with a much larger cast?

Yes. I think it might be a bit messy but I'd certainly be happy to see it tried.

The play's not actually been performed so far?

No. The Royal Shakespeare Company nearly did it with another of my plays they were doing in their festival season, but they were short of rehearsal time and they decided it would be too complicated to do both.

Is there a sequel telling what happens next?

No. Not until I have a child, anyway.

Is Don't Cry Baby *written in the same style as your other work?*

Most of what I write is non-naturalistic. In the case of this play the words came out of those late-night conversations, and the arguments that go round and round in your head – that constant back-and-forth banter. Most of my other plays have been non-naturalistic, and my short stories are more like poetry, really, than novels. Not 'well-made plays' and stories.

What do you mean by 'well-made'? What would a 'well-made' version of Don't Cry Baby *look like on the page, and on the stage?*

The 'well-made play' is a lit.-crit. term. It comes, I think, from nineteenth-century French drama, basically, and describes a play that is well-crafted and realistic. So *Don't Cry Baby* as a 'well-made play' would have four distinct characters, a definite plot and a story line which progresses forward through dialogue and action – the sort of dialogue and action one could see and hear in real life. The story would encompass and overcome obstacles. There would be one major climax or turning point which would resolve the main dilemma of the story. And the play would end with a definite conclusion.

I still think the best plays are well-made . . . Arthur Miller's, say. And the best short stories still have a beginning, a middle and an end. Such forms have evolved over thousands of years: they must satisfy a basic human urge for character, plot, story development, climax and denouement. But I don't usually write 'well-made' plays and stories myself.

Why not?

I'm not good enough? I don't know. Although I believe the old forms – the classic, Aristotelian unities of time, place and action – are the forms which will survive, they don't interest me that much as a writer. Perhaps it's just a phase. At the moment I feel the non-traditional non-naturalistic forms have a greater ability to move an audience. They can carry the emotion, they appeal at a deeper, non-rational level – they can provide a total experience rather than simply a well-constructed argument. On the other hand, our lives and our decisions are made – or at least justified – on the rational level.

What advice have you for a group of young people mounting the world premier of your play? They won't know, first hand, much about the problem of early-middle-aged people wondering if they dare to have a baby, will they?

I think young people are pretty astute. They can see the dilemmas – they can imagine the contradictory pressures. They are ambitious, broody, optimistic, realistic. I'm sure they'll have no trouble identifying with the argument.

My only advice would be to keep it snappy. And enjoy it.

Advertising the play

- Draft the cover for the programme. You could use pencil sketches, cut-outs from magazines, newspaper headlines, baby objects, balloons for what characters say, and any other style or technique that will help.
- Discuss and compare covers.
- Select the cover that will be used.

Bad news comes just as the programme is off to the printers. There is a new TV series just starting, called 'Don't Cry Baby'; it's a silly soap, set in a maternity hospital. You must have a new title. Katie Campbell is unavailable, but her agent says it will be all right if you choose a new title by finding a suitable quotation from the play (as Katie Campbell did).

With ten minutes to the deadline, everybody in the theatre begins to:

- Flick through the script looking for the words (no more than four) that will make a good new title.
- Swap ideas, fast.
- Choose the title.
- Put it on a poster, with suitable illustrations.
- Display it.
- Send it off.

Reading the play

Katie Campbell says the play is 'complicated because the issues are complicated'. Yet the play is easy to 'read' – it has very short speeches and simple vocabulary. How can it be difficult at the same time?

What did *you* find 'complicated' on first reading? What confused you? What still confuses you?

- In small groups, choose a page and read it together.

- Make a list, in order of difficulty, of the five most 'complicated' moments.

- Uncomplicate them by explaining as well as you can what you think is actually going on.

- Compare your complicated moments, and your explanations.

The stage directions at the start of the play say 'rhymes should not be stressed'. Did you even notice there *were* rhymes at the first reading?

The actors can't understand why the playwright bothers with rhymes at all, if they're not to be stressed. The director decides the company need to do some work on rhymes. S/he asks you to work in small groups and:

- Choose two pages.

- Re-read them, disobeying the playwright's instruction and stressing the rhymes as much as possible.

- Re-read the two pages, but this time cut out all the rhymes by inserting new words.

- Brainstorm together (i.e. collect ideas, however odd, as fast as possible) about *rhymes*. (For example, where else do you get rhymes?)

    theatrical entertainments
    songs
    nursery stories
    pantomimes
    adverts

One of you should take notes.

• Each write a three-paragraph note for the theatre programme on 'The poet Katie Campbell's use of rhyme and other poetic devices in her play *Don't Cry Baby*'.

You might begin, 'The use of rhyme in this play is interesting because . . .' Compare notes.

How serious is this play?

• Discuss in small groups and report back.

Look at the playwright's answer to the first question. How serious a problem is having children for her? Do you sympathise with her problem about it? Is it good that women, and to an extent men, can now make *choices* about whether and when to have children?

Does this play explore the question of having or not having children satisfactorily? Are you surprised that adults seem so mixed up about what to do about something so important, and in some ways so easy, as having babies?

Is the humour of the play appropriate? Do the icons, the snappy dialogue, the repetitions and rhymes etc, help? Or does it become a game? Remember that Katie Campbell said 'I wanted the play to be very gymnastic, like child's play or a circus'. Does this work?

Casting the play

You are one of a group of four people who are going to put on a production of *Don't Cry Baby*.

• Argue and discuss with the others in the group how best to cast it.

• Read some passages, varying the casting. Settle on the casting, by votes if necessary.

- Discuss with the other groups how they decided on the casting.
- Choose the best casting from the whole class.

Designing the play

The directions at the beginning of the play say 'Stage is bare except for a crate which is used as a chair, table and bed.'

- Set up this stage.
- Look at it.
- Walk about on it.
- Read some parts of the play on it.

Does the set work? What problems does it raise? What problems does it solve?

- Explore what difference it would make to have different furniture – for example, a real chair, as well, or a bed, or nothing at all.
- Write a paragraph for the theatre programme explaining the slightly unusual setting the playwright asks for. You could start with 'At first, the setting for *Don't Cry Baby* seems . . .

The actors can't understand what the 'icons' are all about. The director sympathises, and says that when you actually *use* them it will be very clear, but first you will do a workshop on 'icons'. In this you have to:

- Read what Katie Campbell says about the icons in the interview (fourth question) and the notes at the start of the play.
- Look up 'icons' in as many reference books as possible. Pool your discoveries.

• In small groups, choose suitable icons for the character in a TV series. For example, a popular Australian series might have a skateboard, a can of lager, an apron, a tube of suntan lotion, and so on.

• Collect four icons for a 'royal family' soap.

• Collect the icons (or 'stand-in' ones) for Katie Campbell's play, and use them while working on some scenes from her play to see what actually happens.

The workshop ends when *everybody* thinks/pretends they're beginning to get the idea of icons.

Exploring the text

• Clip magazines and newspapers for pictures and stories of individuals or groups who seem to you to be relevant to the play, and display all the material.

• Discuss what different items people brought, and why, and what agreements and disagreements there are in the groups.

In order to untangle the play, the director asks you to go through it scene-by-scene and work out what each character thinks about having a baby. S/he suggests you:

• Make a grid, putting a tick when the characters thinks a baby is a good idea in that particular scene, a cross when they think it is a bad idea and a question mark if it's not clear.

For example:

Scenes	1	2	3	4	etc.
Woman	✗	✗	✗	✓	
Man	✓	✗	✗	✓	
Friend	✓	✓	✗	✓	
Mother	✗	✓	✗	✗	

- Compare grids, and what they seem to show.

Katie Campbell said 'I'm sure [young people will] have no trouble identifying with the argument.' Did you?

- Write to the playwright with any difficulties you had. The letter might start like this:

> Dear Katie Campbell,
>
> I am studying your play *Don't Cry Baby*, and there are a few things I do not quite understand. I would be very grateful if you could offer me any explanations to these six problems I still have:
>
> 1 Why don't the characters have names? Real people always do.
>
> 2 . . . etc.

- Write Katie Campbell's reply to your letter.

A 'found' poem is one where you pinch other people's words – perhaps from a newspaper, or adverts, or graffiti, or other poems, or bits of overheard conversation. You are not allowed to make anything up, but you can rearrange and edit, repeat etc. as much as you want.

A 'found' poem based on the preceding paragraph might be:

Overheard

bits of
repeat repeat
bits of other people
overheard found
repeat repeat
as much as you

- *Find* a poem of fifty lines, entitled either 'Not Now', 'Some Other Time' or 'Baby'. All the words must come from Katie Campbell's play.

Katie Campbell explains in the interview what 'well-made' plays and stories are, and why she admires but doesn't write them. Her answer is important evidence, which the director thinks you must understand while working on her play. But the director also realises that nobody does understand, yet. So now there is a workshop on 'well-made plays'.

You are asked to

- Get into pairs and read aloud the questions and answers about 'well-made' plays and stories in Katie Campbell's interview. Jot down what you aren't sure you understand. Ask, look up, discuss. Re-read.

- Then turn over the copy of the interview so that you can't see it, and try to ask the same questions and give the answers. Make up what you can't remember. Check with the original.

- Report back to the other groups your summary of:
  what 'well-made' means
  why anyone might choose to make something that is not 'well-made'.

After the curtain is down

Round a table in the theatre bar after the play, a discussion develops about having babies. 'Would *you* like one?' is the question. Would you?

- First take a vote round the table.

- Say why/why not. (But each person only says one sentence at a time, as in the play – because plays are catching!)

- Discuss the discussion, a sentence at a time. Ask yourselves what has been learned about people's views. Are there any difference in attitudes between male and female, or between those who come from big families and those who don't? How muddled or contradictory are the group's views about having children?

An important person has said that there are too many unimportant people being born, and the world will be too full, and it's time something was done about it.

You are a journalist working for the *Daily Tabloid*, and your editor agrees with the important person's views on eugenics (i.e., the study of improving the human race by selective breeding). The editor asks you to write an article entitled 'Twenty good reasons you haven't thought of for why you shouldn't have children.'

- Write the article. It could start like this:

  1 You are unsuccessful and stupid; if you have a child that'll make two of you.

  2 There are . . .

- Exchange lists and write a (probably angry) letter in reply to the *Daily Tabloid* article, setting out your disagreements with the twenty good reasons you shouldn't have children.

Exchange letters with a partner. You are the letters editor of the *Daily Tabloid*, and of course you do believe in free speech and you do welcome correspondence – but not much of it if it disagrees with the paper's owner's views. So unfortunately you have to shorten the letter to a quarter of its length.

- Do so, making the letter as ineffective as possible.

In another corner of the theatre bar, another discussion is going on about the play between some critics from the newspapers. One of them says that he will write this in his review:

> 'This play is deliberately messy and confusing. Even the title isn't clear.
> Women have been having babies for a long time. What's all the fuss?'

- Continue the review.

Katie Campbell says there is no sequel to her play – 'Not until I have a child, anyway'.

• Write the four-page short story that comes next. (Paragraph one should sum up the play.)

For example:

> 'The man wanted a baby. Her mother and father did, mostly. But she didn't. Then she did. So she did. But that was only the beginning . . .